T·H·E
Authoritative
CALVIN
AND
HOBBES

Other books by Bill Watterson

CALVIN AND HOBBES

SOMETHING UNDER THE BED
IS DROOLING

YUKON HO!

WEIRDOS FROM ANOTHER PLANET

THE CALVIN AND HOBBES
LAZY SUNDAY BOOK

CALVIN AND HOBBES:
REVENGE OF THE BABY-SAT

CALVIN AND HOBBES:
SCIENTIFIC PROGRESS GOES 'BOINK'

CALVIN AND HOBBES:
ATTACK OF THE DERANGED MUTANT KILLER MONSTER
SNOW GOONS

INDISPENSABLE CALVIN AND HOBBES

THE DAYS ARE JUST PACKED

HOMICIDAL PSYCHO JUNGLE CAT

ESSENTIAL CALVIN AND HOBBES

THE CALVIN AND HOBBES TENTH ANNIVERSARY BOOK

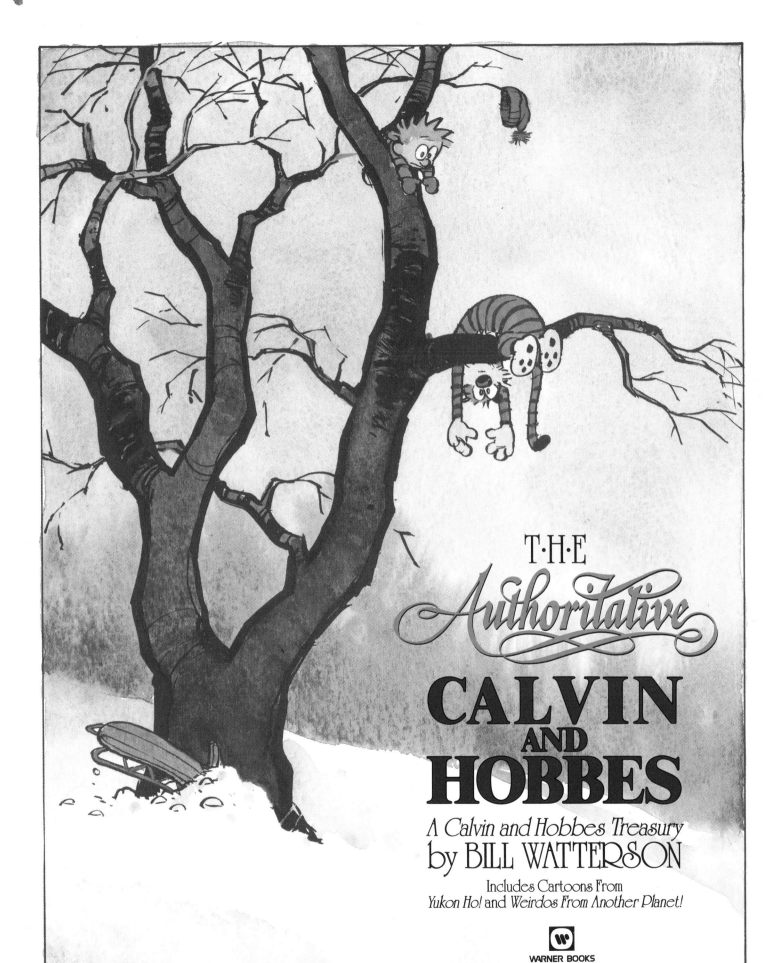

A *Warner* Book

First published in Great Britain by Sphere Books Ltd 1990
Reprinted by Warner Books 1993
Reprinted 1994, 1995, 1996

Copyright © 1990 by Bill Watterson, distributed by
Universal Press Syndicate

The right of Bill Watterson to be identified as
author of this work has been asserted.

Printed and bound in Great Britain by
BPC Books Ltd
A member of
The British Printing Company Ltd

ISBN 0 7515 0795 4

Warner Books
A Division of
Little, Brown and Company (UK)
Brettenham House
Lancaster Place
London WC2E 7EN

To Doctor Dave and
Fellow Moosers John, Brad, and The Frey

CALVIN AND HOBBES by WATTERSON

ARRGH! I'M **NEVER** GOING TO BE ABLE TO MEMORIZE ALL THESE DUMB VOCABULARY WORDS!

TRANSMOG-RIFIER

ZAP
TRANSMOG-RIFIER

HOW CAN ONE LITTLE KID MAKE SO MUCH NOISE?
WUMP WUMP WUMP

CALVIN, WHAT ARE YOU DOING UP THERE?! YOU SOUND LIKE AN ELEPHANT! YOU'RE SUPPOSED TO BE DOING YOUR HOMEWORK!

CALVIN! MY, HOW YOU'VE GROWN SINCE I LAST SAW YOU!

I TRANSMOGRIFIED MYSELF TO FINISH MY HOMEWORK FASTER.

C'MON, LET'S FIND A MUD HOLE TO PLAY IN! ELEPHANTS LOVE MUD!

GREAT! YOU CAN TELL ME SOME ELEPHANT JOKES THERE!

HI CALVIN. BOY, LOOK AT *YOU*!

IMPRESSIVE, EH? HOW DID YOU EVEN RECOGNIZE ME?

I'LL ADMIT IT WASN'T EASY.

HEY, HERE'S A RIDDLE HOBBES MADE UP. WHO DO HOBBES AND I LOOK LIKE? CAN YOU GUESS?

I GIVE UP.

THE REPUBLICAN PARTY AND TAMMANY HALL! SEE? PRETTY GOOD, HUH? HA HA HA HA!

FORGET IT, HOBBES. POLITICAL HUMOR IS JUST TOO SOPHISTICATED FOR GIRLS.

HMPH. HER LOSS!

CALVIN, TIME FOR DINNER!

UH OH. MOM WILL HAVE A FIT IF I GO TO THE TABLE AS AN ELEPHANT.

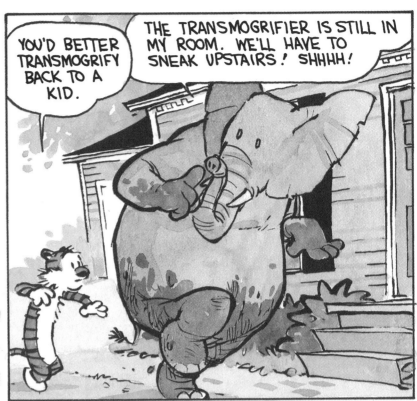

YOU'D BETTER TRANSMOGRIFY BACK TO A KID.

THE TRANSMOGRIFIER IS STILL IN MY ROOM. WE'LL HAVE TO SNEAK UPSTAIRS! SHHHH!

CALVIN, DID I HEAR YOU COME... OH NO!

CALVIN, YOU... AUGHH! WHAT HAVE YOU BEEN DOING?!

IT'S OK, MOM! THIS ISN'T PERMANENT! I WAS JUST GOING TO TRANSMOGRIFY MYSELF BACK TO THE WAY I USED TO BE!

I'LL SAY YOU WILL! WHAT A MESS! GET INTO THE TUB THIS INSTANT!

CALVIN and HOBBES
by WATTERSON

WHEW! THIS MUST BE THE BIGGEST HILL IN THE STATE!

KIND OF FRUSTRATING, ISN'T IT? I WISH DAD WOULD GET TRANSFERRED TO THE ANDES.

LET'S GO DOWN THE HILL AND SEE IF WE CAN TRAVEL INTO THE FUTURE.

GO INTO THE FUTURE? HOW?

IT'S EASY! ALL WE HAVE TO DO IS GET GOING REAL FAST AND WE'LL TIME-WARP!

HA HA! FASTER! FASTER!

GOSH, WHAT DO YOU SUPPOSE THE FUTURE WILL BE LIKE?

WHO KNOWS? FLYING CARS AND CITIES BUILT ON CLOUDS, MAYBE!

JUST THINK OF ALL THE WEIRD THINGS WE CAN TELL PEOPLE WE SAW! OH BOY!

HEY, WE'RE AT THE BOTTOM OF THE HILL. I DIDN'T FEEL ANY TIME WARP, DID YOU?

NOPE.

BUT LOOK! IT'S TWO MINUTES LATER THAN WHEN WE STARTED! WE'RE IN THE FUTURE!!

HMM...THINGS HAVEN'T IMPROVED. I'M DISAPPOINTED.

15

Calvin and Hobbes by WATTERSON

"BEFORE BEGINNING ANY HOME-PLUMBING REPAIR, MAKE SURE YOU POSSESS THE PROPER TOOLS FOR THE JOB."

"CHECK THE FOLLOWING LIST OF HANDY EXPLETIVES, AND SEE THAT YOU KNOW HOW TO USE THEM."

CALVIN WAKES UP ONE MORNING TO FIND HE NO LONGER EXISTS IN THE THIRD DIMENSION! HE IS **2-D**!

THINNER THAN A SHEET OF PAPER, CALVIN HAS NO SURFACE AREA ON THE BOTTOM OF HIS FEET! HE IS IMMOBILE!

ONLY BY "WAVING" HIS BODY CAN CALVIN CREATE ENOUGH FRICTION WITH THE GROUND TO MOVE!

HAVING WIDTH BUT NO THICKNESS, CALVIN IS VULNERABLE TO THE SLIGHTEST GUST OF WIND!

TO AVOID DRAFTS, HE TWISTS HIMSELF INTO A TUBE, AND ROLLS ACROSS THE FLOOR!

SOMEONE IS COMING! CALVIN QUICKLY STANDS UP STRAIGHT.

TURNING PERFECTLY SIDEWAYS, HE IS A NEARLY INVISIBLE VERTICAL LINE! NO ONE WILL NOTICE!

HEY DAD, KNOW WHY YOU DIDN'T SEE ME ALL MORNING?? I WAS TWO-DIMENSIONAL!

HMMM, I'LL BET YOU CAN'T DO IT ALL AFTERNOON, TOO...

DEAR!

I COULDN'T READ IT BECAUSE MY PARENTS FORGOT TO PAY THE GRAVITY BILL.

MAKE A PREDICTION, HOBBES.
WHAT FOR?

SO WE CAN SEE IF YOU HAVE ESP.

OK, I PREDICT YOU'LL FIND AN IRRESISTIBLE ATTRACTION TO A MUD HOLE.

HA HA. YOU STAY AWAY FROM ME.
IT'S GOING TO COME TRUE! I CAN FEEL IT!

HEY DAD, HOW DOES A CARBURETOR WORK?

I CAN'T TELL YOU.

WHY NOT?

IT'S A SECRET.
NO IT ISN'T! YOU JUST DON'T KNOW!

BOMBARDED BY HIGH-ENERGY PHOTONS, CALVIN IS TRANS-FORMED INTO A LIVING X-RAY!

ALTHOUGH THIS CONDITION WILL FACILITATE FUTURE MEDICAL DIAGNOSES, IT DOES MAKE CALVIN'S PRESENCE AT THE DINNER TABLE A DISGUSTING ORDEAL!

EVERYONE CAN SEE CALVIN'S FOOD BEING GROUND INTO MUSHY PULP AND SWALLOWED! AT THIS MOMENT, CALVIN CHEWS UP A LARGE SPOONFUL OF CREAMED CORN!

FOR GOSH SAKES, CLOSE YOUR MOUTH WHEN YOU CHEW!! YOU THINK WE WANT TO *SEE* THAT?!

MKGHH! SMACK! BLAGHKH!

HERE'S A LITTLE TOWN.

HERE'S A STEAMSHOVEL SCOOPING OUT A GIANT HOLE.

HERE COMES THE BULLDOZER, PUSHING THOUSANDS OF BARRELS OF TOXIC NUCLEAR WASTE INTO THE GIANT HOLE.

OVER THE YEARS, THESE DANGEROUS POISONS SEEP INTO UNDERGROUND WATERWAYS.

THE CANCER RATE OF THE NEARBY LITTLE TOWN TRIPLES.

IF YOU WANT ME, I'LL BE UNDER THE BED.

A STRIKE?? THAT PITCH WAS FOUR FEET ABOVE MY HEAD!

HA! IT WAS A *PERFECT* PITCH! YOU'RE JUST TOO SHORT!

YEAH? WELL, *YOU'RE* JUST TOO STUPID!

WELL, YOU'RE JUST TOO *UGLY!*

KICK KICK KICK KICK KICK KI KICK

KICKING DUST IS THE ONLY PART OF THIS GAME WE REALLY LIKE.

I'M GOING OUTSIDE, MOM!

HOLD ALL MY CALLS.

CALVIN LOOKS AROUND. SOMETHING IS DIFFERENT.

THE ODD-COLORED TREE BEHIND HIM SLOWLY LIFTS UP! IT'S NOT A TREE AT ALL! IT'S A LEG!

OH NO! CALVIN IS THE SIZE OF A BUG *TO* A BUG! HE RUNS FOR HIS LIFE!

A CLAW CRASHES WITH DEAFENING IMPACT! THE BUG IS TRYING TO STEP ON CALVIN! WHAT A HORRIBLE FATE!

CALVIN SCRAMBLES MADLY, PROMISING HIMSELF THAT HE'LL NEVER SQUISH ANOTHER BUG IF HE LIVES TO RETURN TO NORMAL SIZE!

SUDDENLY IN A SPRAY OF SLIME, THE BUG IS GONE! A MONSTROUS FROG LICKS ITS CHOPS! CALVIN IS SAVED!

AACCK! WHAT'S THAT ON MY PLATE?! GOOD HEAVENS, GET IT OFF THE TABLE!!

BUT MOM, FROGS ARE OUR *FRIENDS!*

24

OK, I THINK THAT'S DAD'S BUILDING UP AHEAD.

I'M NOT SURE WHERE HIS OFFICE IS, SO WE'LL JUST HAVE TO LOOK IN THE WINDOWS AS WE ZIP BY.

HEY! THERE HE IS! THERE'S DAD! HI, DAD! DAD, LOOK! OUT THE WINDOW!!

DARN IT! HE'S STILL READING THAT BRIEF. LOOK OUT THE WINDOW, DAD!

DID YOU BRING ANY ROCKS? I DIDN'T THINK TO.

HEY DAD! LOOK OUT THE WINDOW! ...I CAN'T BELIEVE HE'S JUST SITTING IN THERE.

WHY DOESN'T HE LOOK UP?

I GUESS HE'S PRETTY BUSY.

YEAH, BUT WE CAN'T SIT UP HERE ALL DAY! SHEESH. LET'S GO.

IF HE HAD NOTICED US, WE COULD'VE GIVEN HIM A RIDE HOME.

HMPH. I SAY LET HIM TAKE THE SMELLY OL' BUS IF HE CAN'T EVEN LOOK OUT THE WINDOW ONCE IN A WHILE. SERVES HIM RIGHT.

I'M HOME!

DAD! HOBBES AND I FLEW BY YOUR OFFICE WINDOW TODAY ON A RUG! WE SAW YOU WORKING.

WE WAVED AND HOLLERED, BUT YOU DIDN'T EVEN LOOK UP. WE COULDN'T BELIEVE IT. YOU MISSED THE WHOLE THING!

I THOUGHT WE WERE CUTTING DOWN HIS SUGAR INTAKE.

Calvin and Hobbes by Watterson

OY OH BOY OH BOY OH BOY OH BOY OH BOY OH BOY OH BOY OH BOY OH BOY

WAIT! WAIT! I'VE GOT TO SAVOR THIS MOMENT! THE BRILLIANCE OF IT ALL! I'M A GENIUS! A SHEER *GENIUS!*

SUSIE'S PLAYING ON THE SIDEWALK! NOW'S MY CHANCE TO USE THE SNOW-BALL I'VE BEEN SAVING IN THE FREEZER!

SHE'LL NEVER EXPECT A SNOW-BALL IN *JUNE!* BOY, WILL SHE BE MAD! HA HA HA!

THIS IS GOING TO BE GREAT! HERE IT COMES! OH BOY! OH BOY!

HEY SUSIE!!

PIFF

WATTERSON

I *MISSED!* DARN IT DARN IT DARN IT!! OF ALL THE MISERABLE LUCK!

AAARRGHH!

THERE MUST'VE BEEN A CROSS BREEZE! I CAN'T BELIEVE IT! I SAVED THAT SNOWBALL FOR THREE WHOLE MONTHS! I...

SCOOP SCOOP

I.. I...UH...

POW

THE IRONY OF THIS IS JUST SICKENING.

1988 ISN'T TOO FAR AWAY, DAD.

IF YOU'RE THINKING OF RUNNING FOR "DAD" AGAIN, YOU'D BETTER GET YOUR CAMPAIGN IN GEAR.

FRANKLY, THE POLLS LOOK GRIM. I DON'T THINK YOU'VE GOT MUCH OF A SHOT AT KEEPING THE OFFICE.

I TAKE COMFORT IN THE FACT THAT NOT MANY PEOPLE WOULD WANT IT.

FLIPPANT REMARKS HAVE A WAY OF HAUNTING CANDIDATES, YOU KNOW.

THE CHAMELEON SITS MOTIONLESS.

AMAZINGLY, THE LIZARD CHANGES COLOR TO BLEND IN WITH HIS SURROUNDINGS.

MOMENTS LATER, HE IS VIRTUALLY INVISIBLE.

I SEE YOU HIDING BACK THERE! NOW COME CLEAN UP THIS MESS YOU MADE IN THE KITCHEN!

HOLD STILL. THERE'S A MONSTER HORSEFLY ON YOUR HEAD.

POW!!

CAN YOU BELIEVE IT? I MISSED!

!

SO EXCUSE ME FOR TRYING TO HELP! YOU WANNA SCRATCH A STINGING WELT ALL DAY? FINE! GO AWAY!

NO, WAIT. THERE'S A MOSQUITO ON YOU.

31

CALVIN and HOBBES

by WATTERSON

THE DREADED SCUM BEINGS FIRE! SPACEMAN SPIFF IS *HIT!*

IT NEVER FAILS. I JUST WASHED AND WAXED THIS THING.

OUR HERO, THE INTREPID SPACEMAN SPIFF, STRUGGLES WITH THE CONTROLS OF HIS DAMAGED SPACECRAFT!

THE FREEM PROPULSION BLASTERS ARE USELESS! SPIFF CRASHES ONTO THE SURFACE OF AN ALIEN PLANET!

UNSCATHED, THE FEARLESS SPACE EXPLORER EMERGES FROM THE SMOLDERING WRECKAGE! HE IS MAROONED ON A HOSTILE WORLD!

SCORCHED BY TWIN SUNS, THE PLANET IS NOTHING BUT BARREN ROCK AND METHANE! THERE'S NO HOPE OF FINDING FOOD OR WATER!

SPIFF COLLAPSES! OH NO, A HIDEOUS ALIEN SPOTS HIM! IN HIS WEAKENED STATE, SPIFF IS NO MATCH FOR THE MONSTER! *THIS COULD BE THE END!!*

WATTERSON

LUNCHTIME! I BROUGHT YOU A SANDWICH AND SOME LEMONADE.

BRING THE DISHES BACK WHEN YOU'RE DONE, OK?

...OH WELL.

THANKS, MOM.

QUICK, MOM! ALIENS JUST LANDED IN THE BACK YARD! THEY DEMAND TO TALK TO YOU!

YOU GO ON OUT! I'LL GUARD THE COOKIES IN THE KITCHEN!

QUICK! HURRY!

SHE'S NOT BUYING THIS.

CALVIN, JUST HOW DUMB DO YOU THINK I AM?

WHAT DO YOU THINK IS THE SECRET TO HAPPINESS? IS IT MONEY, POWER OR FAME?

I'D CHOOSE MONEY. IF YOU HAVE ENOUGH MONEY, YOU CAN BUY POWER AND FAME. THAT WAY YOU'D HAVE IT ALL AND BE REALLY HAPPY!

HAPPINESS IS BEING FAMOUS FOR YOUR FINANCIAL ABILITY TO INDULGE IN EVERY KIND OF EXCESS.

I SUPPOSE THAT'S ONE WAY TO DEFINE IT.

THE PART I THINK I'D LIKE BEST IS CRUSHING PEOPLE WHO GET IN MY WAY.

LOOK! SOMEBODY POURED NEW CEMENT!

IS ANYONE LOOKING? WE COULD WRITE OUR INITIALS IN IT, OR MAKE A HAND PRINT, OR SOMETHING!

YEAH! "OR SOMETHING"!

I THINK WE'D BETTER FIND A HOSE QUICK!

I DIDN'T THINK IT WOULD SET UP SO FAST.

Calvin and Hobbes
by WATTERSON

PSST... HEY, KID. C'MERE UNDER THE BED. I'VE GOT A BRAND NEW TOY FOR YOU.

UH OH. I THINK I SAW A TENTACLE UNDER THE BED!

MONSTERS!

TURN ON THE LIGHTS! THAT MAKES MONSTERS SHRIVEL UP.

GOOD IDEA.

CLICK!

AARRGHHH! AIEEEE AAHHHHHH!! GAACKK

HA HA. WE GOT 'EM!

JUST THE ONES UNDER THE BED. WE'D BETTER OPEN UP THE DRAWERS AND CLOSET TOO, AND GET SOME LIGHT IN THOSE PLACES!

BY GOLLY, NO MONSTERS ARE GOING TO GET US TONIGHT! WITHER AND DIE, BLOODSUCKING FREAKS OF NATURE!!

WHY IS YOUR LIGHT ON? WHAT IN THE WORLD ARE YOU DOING ?!?

MONSTERS, DAD. THEY COULD BE ANYWHERE.

YOU'RE TRASHING YOUR ROOM AT 1:00 IN THE MORNING, LOOKING FOR MONSTERS?! IF YOU DON'T GET IN BED THIS INSTANT, YOU'LL HAVE A LOT MORE TO WORRY ABOUT THAN STUPID MONSTERS!!

...WHAT WE NEED IS SOME WAY TO SHRIVEL HIM UP.

HEY CALVIN, WHATCHA DOIN'?

SHHH!

QUIET DOWN OR YOU'LL GIVE AWAY MY POSITION. HOBBES AND I ARE HAVING A WATER FIGHT.

A WATER FIGHT! CAN I PLAY?

YOU? HA! WAR IS A *MANLY* ART!

I SUPPOSE ANYTHING SO IDIOTIC WOULD *HAVE* TO BE. CAN I PLAY IN YOUR GAME OR NOT?

I DON'T KNOW, IT SEEMS YOU'D RATHER BE MAKING SMART REMARKS.

C'MON, CAN'T I JOIN YOUR WATER FIGHT? I HAVE MY OWN WATER PISTOL AND EVERYTHING! IT'LL JUST TAKE ME A MINUTE TO GET IT.

OK, YOU CAN PLAY, BUT HOBBES IS ON *MY* TEAM. YOU HAVE TO FIGHT BOTH OF US.

WATTERSON

GREAT! I CAN BEAT YOU AND YOUR STUFFED TIGER ANY DAY. I'LL GO PUT ON MY SWIMSUIT.

SUSIE'S GOING TO PLAY WITH US, OK?

OH BOY, GIRLS FLIP FOR GUYS IN JAMS.

I GOT MY WATER PISTOL! I'M ALL SET!

GOOD. NOW HOBBES AND I WILL BE ONE TEAM, AND YOU...

LOOK AT YOUR TOY TIGER! HE'S WEARING *JAMS*!! THAT'S SO *CUTE*! LET ME SQUEEZE HIM!

OH FOR PETE'S SAKE, KNOCK IT OFF! YOU GO AROUND THE HOUSE AND COUNT TO FIFTY, AND THEN WE BEGIN, ALL RIGHT?

YOU AND YOUR DUMB JAMS. THIS IS *WAR*, REMEMBER?!

YOU'RE JUST JEALOUS. ...OOH, WHAT A BABE!

LISTEN UP, YOGURT BRAIN. HERE'S OUR STRATEGY: I'LL GO AROUND THE HOUSE *THIS* WAY, AND YOU GO AROUND THE *OTHER* WAY.

I'LL DRAW SUSIE'S FIRE, AND YOU CAN LET HER HAVE IT FROM BEHIND WITH YOUR WATER BALLOON!

GOT IT? OK, LET'S GO!

THANKS FOR THE WATER BALLOON, HOBBES. YOU'RE A GREAT DOUBLE AGENT!

HA HA! AMBUSH!! HAVE A DRINK, SUSIE!

WHOA! WHOOP! YOU'VE GOT HOBBES' WATER BALLOON! WHERE DID...? HOW...? ..UH OH..

BLOOSH!

I PROMISE YOU YOU'LL HANG FOR THIS, TRAITOR!

I'M EASILY WILED BY A WOMAN IN A SWIMSUIT.

MY BEST FRIEND BETRAYS ME! SUSIE DRENCHED ME WITH MY OWN TEAMMATE'S WATER BALLOON!

SOME BUDDY *YOU* ARE, YOU BENEDICT ARNOLD!

HMPH. I'D DO IT AGAIN IN A MINUTE. SUSIE LIKES MY JAMS.

DON'T EVEN TALK TO ME! YOU AND I ARE THROUGH!

HA! PROMISES, PROMISES!

UM... I TAKE IT THE GAME IS OVER.

GET THIS TRAITOR OFF ME. HE CHEATS WHEN HE FIGHTS, TOO.

Calvin and Hobbes
by WATTERSON

CAN YOU BELIEVE THIS? SOME IDIOT TOSSED GARBAGE HERE IN THIS BEAUTIFUL SPOT.

I'LL BET FUTURE CIVILIZATIONS FIND OUT MORE ABOUT US THAN WE'D LIKE THEM TO KNOW.

LOOK, ANOTHER CAN THROWN ON THE GROUND! BOY, THIS MAKES ME MAD!

BY GOLLY, IF PEOPLE AREN'T BURYING TOXIC WASTES OR TESTING NUCLEAR WEAPONS, THEY'RE THROWING TRASH EVERYWHERE!

YOU'D THINK PLANETS LIKE THIS WERE A DIME A DOZEN! NOW *I'VE* GOT TO CARRY THIS GROSS THING.

YOU KNOW, THERE ARE TIMES WHEN IT'S A SOURCE OF PERSONAL PRIDE TO NOT BE HUMAN.

I'M WITH YOU.

AREN'T THESE LONG SUMMER DAYS GREAT? NO RESPONSIBILITIES AT ALL! WE HAVE THE WHOLE DAY TO OURSELVES.

DON'T YOU WISH IT COULD BE LIKE THIS ALL YEAR, FOREVER? NO SCHOOL, NO JOB, NO ANYTHING?

YEAH, JUST GLOAT ABOUT IT, WHY DON'T YOU!!

HEY DAD, WHAT ARE CLOUDS MADE OF?

HMM... I USED TO KNOW THAT. I THINK THEY'RE MOSTLY WATER.

SO HOW COME THEY FLOAT?

WELL, IT'S SORT OF EVAPORATED WATER. MAYBE THERE ARE SOME OTHER GASES, TOO. I'M NOT SURE.

SO WHY ARE THEY WHITE WHEN THE REST OF THE SKY IS BLUE?

HECK, BEATS ME. I GUESS WE OUGHT TO LOOK THIS STUFF UP.

I TAKE IT THERE'S NO QUALIFYING EXAM TO BE A DAD.

ONE OF THE BEST THINGS ABOUT SUMMER IS GOING TO SLEEP WITH THE FAN ON.

THE GENTLE BREEZE BLOWING, THE DRONING HUM...EVERYTHING SEEMS SAFE AND SERENE WHEN THE FAN IS ON.

IT'S COOL AND LULLING AND PERFECT FOR SLEEP.

IT ALMOST LETS ONE FORGET HE HAS A HEAVY FUR COAT FOR A BUNKMATE.

IF YOU DON'T LIKE IT, THERE'S PLENTY OF ROOM ON THE FLOOR, BUSTER.

Calvin: HEY MOM, WHAT'S THIS I HEAR ABOUT THE GREENHOUSE EFFECT?

Calvin: THEY SAY THE POLLUTANTS WE DUMP IN THE AIR ARE TRAPPING IN THE SUN'S HEAT AND IT'S GOING TO MELT THE POLAR ICE CAPS!

Calvin: SURE, *YOU'LL* BE GONE WHEN IT HAPPENS, BUT *I* WON'T! NICE PLANET YOU'RE LEAVING ME!

Mom: THIS FROM THE KID WHO WANTS TO BE CHAUFFEURED ANY PLACE MORE THAN A BLOCK AWAY.

Calvin: HEY, NOBODY TOLD ME ABOUT THE ICE CAPS, ALL RIGHT?

Calvin: MORE BAD NEWS ON YOUR POLLS, DAD. WE'RE LOOKING AT AN ALL-TIME LOW IN POPULARITY HERE.

Dad: WELL, CALVIN, THAT'S CERTAINLY FOOD FOR THOUGHT.

Calvin: NOW HERE'S SOMETHING *YOU* CAN THINK ABOUT. THE AVERAGE COST OF RAISING A KID TO AGE 18 IS $100,000. THAT'S A LOT OF MONEY.

Calvin: SO THE QUESTION YOU SHOULD BE ASKING YOURSELF IS, "IS THAT HUNDRED GRAND A *GIFT*... OR A *LOAN*?"

Dad: GOTCHA, DAD. I WAS JUST ON MY WAY TO BED.

RING RING

Calvin: HELLO?

Voice: MAY I SPEAK WITH YOUR FATHER, PLEASE?

Calvin: HECK, YOU DON'T NEED *MY* PERMISSION! BE MY GUEST!

Calvin: WHAT A WEIRDO.

RING RING

41

Panel 1: DEEP IN A DANK DUNGEON ON THE DISMAL PLANET ZOG, THE FEARLESS SPACEMAN SPIFF IS HELD PRISONER BY THE SINISTER ZOG KING.

Panel 2: A GUARD LEADS SPIFF TO THE INTERROGATION ROOM. OUR HERO IS STOIC AND DEFIANT!

Panel 3: AT LAST I MEET THE FAMED SPACEMAN SPIFF! I TRUST YOU ARE...HEH HEH... ENJOYING YOUR VISIT?

YOU'RE WASTING YOUR TIME, MAGGOT FROM MARS! I'LL NEVER GIVE IN!

Panel 4: NEVER, YOU HEAR ME?! *NEVER!*

KID, DON'T MAKE ME RECANT THE HIPPOCRATIC OATH, OK?

Panel 5: WELL, YOU CERTAINLY WERE A TERROR IN THE DOCTOR'S OFFICE.

Panel 6: I FENDED HIM OFF WITH HIS OWN TONGUE DEPRESSOR. THAT'S WHY I DIDN'T GET A SHOT.

YOU DIDN'T *NEED* A SHOT. YOUR BEHAVIOR WAS INEXCUSABLE.

Panel 7: ALL THAT COUNTS IS THAT HE COULDN'T GET NEAR ENOUGH TO STICK ME. HE THINKS I'M A LITTLE PINK PIN CUSHION IN UNDERPANTS.

Panel 8: SOMEDAY I HOPE YOU HAVE A KID THAT PUTS YOU THROUGH WHAT I'VE GONE THROUGH.

YEAH, GRANDMA SAYS THAT'S WHAT SHE USED TO TELL *YOU.*

Panel 9: HERE IS A PROUD CITY, FULL OF HAPPY, PROSPEROUS CITIZENS.

Panel 10: THEY GO ON ABOUT THEIR BUSINESS, **UNAWARE** THAT THE MOON HAS MYSTERIOUSLY MOVED A FEW MILES CLOSER TO THE EARTH.

Panel 11: ...UNAWARE, THAT IS, UNTIL THE TIDE COMES IN.

Panel 12: SPLOOSH! GISSHHH!

CALVIN and HOBBES by WATTERSON

THE FIRE'S NOT LIGHTING, HUH? CAN I MAKE A SUGGESTION?

GIVE UP ON THAT SISSY LIGHTER FLUID.

CAN'T WE COOK THE HAMBURGERS YET?

THE COALS AREN'T HOT ENOUGH.

BUT I'M HUNGRY! I WANT TO EAT *NOW!*

WELL, YOU'LL JUST HAVE TO WAIT.

YOU KNOW, CALVIN, SOMETIMES THE ANTICIPATION OF SOMETHING IS MORE FUN THAN THE THING ITSELF ONCE YOU GET IT.

HERE WE ARE, IT'S A BEAUTIFUL EVENING. IT'S NICE TO JUST SIT HERE AND LOOK AT THE TREES WHILE WE WAIT FOR THE COALS TO GET HOT, DON'T YOU THINK?

DINNER WILL BE OVER SOON, AND AFTERWARD WE'LL BE DISTRACTED WITH OTHER THINGS TO DO. BUT NOW WE HAVE A FEW MINUTES TO OURSELVES TO ENJOY THE EVENING.

THESE SUMMER DAYS GO BY SO QUICKLY. IT'S GOOD THAT EVERY NOW AND THEN WE HAVE TO WAIT FOR SOMETHING.

SO SHOULD I GO TO McDONALD'S THEN, OR WHAT?

YEAH, I KNOW. YOU THINK YOU'RE GOING TO BE SIX ALL YOUR LIFE.

WHAT A PERFECT DAY!

ISN'T IT GREAT TO BE ON SUMMER VACATION? TO BE ABLE TO ENJOY ALL THIS WITH NO SCHOOL AND NO RESPONSIBILITIES?

..AHHHHHHH...

I CAN'T BELIEVE THERE'S NOTHING ON TV BUT REPEATS.

I THINK A BEE LANDED ON MY BACK! CAN YOU SEE IT? I DON'T WANT TO MOVE!

THAT'S NOT A BEE.

IT ISN'T? *WHEW*

NO, THAT'S A HORNET IF I EVER SAW ONE!

OW!

Calvin and Hobbes

by WATTERSON

WIPE THAT GRIN OFF YOUR FACE!

WELL, HOBBES, HOW DO I LOOK?

I'M DOING MY BEST TO BITE MY TONGUE.

I CUT OUT CONSTRUCTION PAPER FEATHERS AND TAPED THEM ON MY ARMS SO I CAN FLY! PRETTY NEAT, HUH?

IF PAPER FEATHERS ARE ALL IT TAKES TO FLY, DON'T YOU THINK WE'D HAVE HEARD ABOUT IT BEFORE?

IT TAKES AN UNCOMMON MIND TO THINK OF THESE THINGS, HOBBES.

I'D AGREE WITH THAT.

HERE'S A GORGE. THIS IS A GOOD SPOT.

YOU'RE GOING TO JUMP OFF THIS LEDGE?

HECK NO! I NEED *MOMENTUM!* I WANT YOU TO *TOSS* ME OVER.

YOU UNDERSTAND I ASSUME NO RESPONSIBILITY FOR THIS?

RIGHT. *I* GET THE PATENT.

HEAVE!

I'M FLYING! I'M FLYING!

I'M..... UH OH...

DON'T SELL THE BIKE SHOP, ORVILLE.

SHUT UP AND GO GET ME SOME ANTISEPTIC.

CalViN and HobbES
by WATTERSON

THAT RUN DOESN'T COUNT! YOU DIDN'T TOUCH THIRD BASE!

THAT'S 'CAUSE THIRD BASE CRAWLED TO THE OUTFIELD!

WAP!

HA HA! EASY OUT!!

HEY! WHERE ARE YOU GOING?!

YOU HAVE TO STAY ON THE BASE LINE, YOU CHEATER!

YEAH? PROVE IT!

THIS ISN'T FAIR! YOU CAN'T RUN ANYWHERE!

JUST WATCH ME!

IF WE HAD A FIRST BASEMAN, YOU'D'VE BEEN OUT LONG AGO!

BUT WE DON'T, DO WE?

GOTCHA! YOU'RE OUT!

OK, I'M UP TO BAT AGAIN! WHAT FUN! TWO-MAN BASEBALL IS A REAL SPORT!

A REAL SPORT FOR IDIOTS. NEXT TIME I'M GOING TO TAG YOU OUT WITH THE BAT INSTEAD OF THE BALL.

48

HOBBES, DID YOU HEAR? MOM AND DAD ARE TAKING US CAMPING!

WE GET TO LIVE IN A TENT AND GO FISHING AND CANOEING! WON'T THAT BE **FUN**??

WATTERSON

WE'LL BE ROUGHING IT! LIVING OFF THE LAND! NO TV OR RADIO OR....

UH-OH.

WHAT'S WRONG?

THIS SOUNDS SUSPICIOUSLY LIKE ONE OF DAD'S PLOTS TO BUILD MY CHARACTER.

GOSH, THIS IS GOING TO BE A **FUN** VACATION! CAMPING OUT! WOW!

WATTERSON

I CAN'T WAIT TO GET THERE! A WHOLE WEEK OF HIKING AND CANOEING AND SWIMMING AND FISHING!

A WHOLE WEEK WITHOUT A SINGLE NEWSPAPER OR A DECENT CUP OF REAL COFFEE.

DOESN'T MOM **LIKE** CAMPING?

MOM WAS UP A LITTLE TOO LATE PACKING.

SEE THAT ISLAND UP AHEAD? THAT'S WHERE WE'RE CAMPING!

OH BOY!

AHH, THIS IS THE LIFE! FRESH AIR, CLEAN WATER, LOTS OF EXERCISE, AND...

BOOM!

DEAR, YOU'RE BACK-PADDLING.

WE'RE TURNING AROUND AND FINDING A HOTEL!

WATTERSON

CALVIN and HOBBES by WATERSON

TUM DE TA TA DEE DEE DO

BOY, THIS SURE BEATS SITTING IN AN OFFICE ALL DAY!

IS IT STILL RAINING?

OF COURSE IT'S STILL RAINING. IT'S BEEN RAINING FOR DAYS. WHY SHOULD IT STOP NOW?!

WE'RE GOING TO NEED A VACATION AFTER *THIS* VACATION.

I'LL SAY! WE CAN'T EVEN KEEP A FIRE GOING.

I CAN'T BELIEVE DAD WENT OUT TO CATCH FISH.

IN *THIS* WEATHER? HE'S A FANATIC!

EITHER THAT, OR WE'RE ALL OUT OF PACKAGED FOOD. WE'LL PROBABLY STARVE TO DEATH ON THIS GOD-FORSAKEN ROCK.

AFTER ALL THAT SPAM, STARVING DOESN'T SOUND SO BAD.

IF WE LIVE TO GET HOME, I'M NEVER GOING TO SET FOOT OUTSIDE AGAIN AS LONG AS I LIVE.

WHAT A LUCKY KID CALVIN IS! I NEVER GOT TO DO THIS STUFF WHEN *I* WAS HIS AGE!

HEY CALVIN! WANT TO LEARN HOW TO GUT A FISH?

WELL, GANG, I'M SORRY THE WEATHER WASN'T ANY BETTER THIS WEEK.

I KNOW IT WASN'T ALWAYS A LOT OF FUN, BUT WE LIVED THROUGH IT, AND WE GOT TO SPEND SOME TIME TOGETHER, AND THAT'S WHAT'S REALLY IMPORTANT.

ANYWAY, I HOPE YOU'RE ALL NOT *TOO* DISAPPOINTED.

CALVIN, TELL YOUR DAD ANY JUDGE WOULD TAKE THIS TRIP AS GROUNDS FOR DIVORCE.

DAD, MOM SAYS...

ALL RIGHT! ALL RIGHT!

DAD, CAN YOU GET MY BALL OUT OF THE GUTTER AGAIN?

THIS IS THE THIRD TIME THIS AFTERNOON! I THOUGHT I TOLD YOU TO PLAY OUT BACK!

RELAX, DAD. IT'S JUST A BALL IN THE GUTTER. IT'S NOT AS IF I'VE BEEN EMBEZZLING MONEY OR KILLING PEOPLE, RIGHT? AREN'T YOU GLAD I'M NOT STEALING AND MURDERING?

I ALWAYS HAVE TO HELP DAD ESTABLISH THE PROPER CONTEXT.

C'MON, HOBBES. LET DOWN THE ROPE LADDER.

WHAT'S THE REST OF THE PASSWORD?

I THINK FIVE VERSES EXTOLLING TIGERS IS *PLENTY*. YOU KNOW IT'S ME! LET ME UP!

NO.

OOH, WHY YOU LOUSY, ROTTEN, STINKING..

IF YOU CALL ME NAMES, YOU HAVE TO START OVER AT THE BEGINNING.

VERSE SIX: "TIGERS ARE NIMBLE AND LIGHT ON THEIR TOES, MY *RE*SPECT FOR TIGERS CONTINUALLY GROWS."

YOU'RE NOT DOING THE DANCE.

Calvin and Hobbes by Watterson

AH-CHOO!

WHEW ...NO BRAINS.

AH.. AH.. AH.. **AH**

CHOOO!

THE FORCE OF THE NASAL EXPLOSION SENDS CALVIN REELING THROUGH THE STRATOSPHERE!

WITH LESS AND LESS AIR TO RESIST HIS MOMENTUM, HE BREAKS THE PULL OF EARTH'S GRAVITY AND HURLS PAST THE MOON!

AS HE PASSES OUT OF THE GALAXY, CALVIN REFLECTS ON THE WISDOM OF COVERING ONE'S MOUTH WHEN SNEEZING TO DEFLECT THE PROPULSION.

ALAS, IT IS KNOWLEDGE GAINED TOO LATE FOR POOR CALVIN, THE HUMAN SATELLITE! ...BUT WAIT! ANOTHER SNEEZE IS BREWING! CALVIN TURNS HIMSELF AROUND!

THE SECOND SNEEZE ROCKETS HIM BACK TO EARTH! HE'S SAVED! IT'S A MIRACLE!

AH CHOO!

GOD BLESS YOU.

OH, HE *DOES*, MOM. HE *DOES*.

THE END OF SUMMER IS ALWAYS HARD ON ME.

...TRYING TO CRAM IN ALL THE GOOFING OFF I'VE BEEN MEANING TO DO.

HOW COME YOU'RE STILL HOME? WHY AREN'T YOU AT WORK?

I TOOK THE DAY OFF.

SAY, DAD, CAN I HAVE A LOOK AT THE CLASSIFIED SECTION?

AS SOON AS I'M THROUGH WITH IT.

GOSH, DAD, I'D SURE LIKE TO BORROW THAT SECTION RIGHT THIS MINUTE. WHY DON'T YOU READ THE EDITORIALS?

"NEW DAD WANTED. FREQUENT TRAVELER PREFERRED. LIBERAL VIEWS ON DISCIPLINE A MUST. ASK FOR CALVIN DURING NORMAL WORK HOURS"

I DON'T *WANNA* TAKE A BATH! I *HATE* TAKING BATHS!

AAAAAAAAAAAH

NO NO NO NO NO NO NO NO NO NO NO NO NO

THEY CAN MAKE ME DO IT, BUT THEY CAN'T MAKE ME DO IT WITH DIGNITY.

RATS. I CAN'T TELL MY GUM FROM MY SILLY PUTTY.

WAP WAP WAP WAP

WIPPITY WAPPITY WIPPITY WAPPITY

BIPPITABIPPITABIPPITABIPPITABIPPITA

I'M NEVER GONNA GET MARRIED. ARE YOU?

HMM... I SUPPOSE IF THE RIGHT PERSON CAME ALONG, I MIGHT.

SOMEBODY WITH GREEN EYES AND A NICE LAUGH, WHO I COULD CALL "POOTY PIE."

"POOTY PIE"?!?

OR "BITSY POOKUMS."

I THINK THAT WOULD AFFECT MY STOMACH A LOT MORE THAN MY HEART.

"BITSY POOKUMS," I'D SAY. "YES, SNOOGY WOOGY," SHE'D REPLY...

CalviN and HobbEs

by WATTERSON

STIR STIR · STRETTCCHHH · STAB STAB · PAT PAT PAT · MUSH MUSH · SNIFF

HWOOF! · LICK · ACKPTGH · BLECHH · GLUG GLUG GLUG · SMACK · BR-R-R-R-R

HAAAKK HOCCHH

CHOKE... GASP...

THERE...(PANT)... SEE?
I...I...*TRIED* IT. (COUGH)
IT... ALMOST (WHEEZE)
KILLED... ME.

CLAP CLAP **CLAP** CLAP CL
ENCORE. · BRA**VO**.
I'M GOING TO RUN AWAY TO ALASKA.

WE MADE IT! IT'S A GOOD THING THE TIME MACHINE DIDN'T STALL, OR WE'D HAVE BEEN EATEN BY DINOSAURS!

WE'RE COMING BACK TOWARD THE PRESENT NOW. DO YOU WANT TO STOP AT HOME, OR KEEP GOING INTO THE FUTURE LIKE WE PLANNED?

I'VE HAD ENOUGH TIME TRAVELING. LET'S GO HOME.

LET'S GO JUST A *LITTLE* INTO THE FUTURE AND SEE WHAT I'M LIKE AS A TEEN-AGER!

LET'S NOT, ALL RIGHT?

HI, MOM. HOBBES AND I WENT TIME TRAVELING AND VISITED THE JURASSIC PERIOD TODAY.

THAT'S NICE. WHAT'S IT LIKE?

PRETTY SCARY. A DINOSAUR ALMOST ATE US.

ACTUALLY, WE WERE TRYING TO GO INTO THE FUTURE, BUT WE MADE A MISTAKE.

I SEE. WELL, I'M GLAD YOU MADE IT BACK.

YOUR MOM ISN'T FAZED BY MUCH, IS SHE?

IT DEPENDS. SHE DIDN'T TAKE THE FROGS IN THE TOILET SO WELL, REMEMBER?

DAD, LOOK! THE SUN'S SETTING AND IT'S ONLY 3 O'CLOCK!

IT'S NOT 3 O'CLOCK. YOUR WATCH STOPPED.

TIME DOESN'T STOP IF YOUR WATCH STOPS?

NOPE.

PHOOEY. FOR A MOMENT THERE, I THOUGHT I'D GET RICH PATENTING THIS THING.

I'D HAVE BOUGHT ONE.

IF YOU COULD HAVE THREE WISHES GRANTED, WHAT WOULD THEY BE?

JUST THREE WISHES, HUH? HMM... THAT WOULD BE A TOUGH DECISION.

I GUESS I'D HAVE TO THINK ABOUT IT A WHILE.

OOPS! HANG ON.

OK, I KNOW WHAT MY FIRST WISH WOULD BE.

ONE OF NATURE'S UGLIER CREATURES, THE BAT IS A MISUNDERSTOOD MARVEL OF EVOLUTION.

PRODUCING A SERIES OF LOUD, HIGH-PITCHED SQUEAKS, THE BAT CAN JUDGE AN INSECT'S DISTANCE AND ELEVATION BY THE TIME DELAY OF THE SQUEAK'S ECHO!

CHANGES IN THE ECHO'S PITCH REVEAL THE DOOMED BUG'S DIRECTION! NO MOVEMENT ESCAPES THE INCREDIBLE SENSES OF THE BAT!

GLUMP!

TA-DAA! EYES CLOSED!

CALVIN, SIT UP AND EAT WITH A FORK LIKE A CIVILIZED HUMAN BEING.

YAWN

WAAUUGHH!

FOR THE LAST TIME, GET OUT OF BED! WE'RE GOING TO BE LATE.

I'M TRYING. I'M TRYING.

GOSH, MAYBE MOM AND DAD SOLD ALL MY BELONGINGS WHEN I SECEDED.

MAYBE THEY RENTED OUT MY ROOM.

MAYBE THEY *MOVED!*

...A LOT CAN HAPPEN WHEN YOU'RE GONE ALL MORNING! *...MOMMMM!!*

I'M BACK, MOM. I CHANGED MY MIND ABOUT SECEDING. I WANT TO BE YOUR KID AGAIN, OK?

YOU'LL ALWAYS BE MY KID. I'M GLAD YOU'RE BACK.

WELL, HOBBES WAS BEING A MORON, SO I DECIDED I DIDN'T WANT TO LIVE IN THE YUKON WITH HIM.

SO WHERE IS HOBBES NOW?

ISN'T HE BACK YET?

HOW COULD HOBBES GET BACK BY HIMSELF?!

YOU'RE RIGHT. THAT DUMB TIGER COULDN'T FIND HIS WAY OUT OF AN EMPTY ROOM.

BEDTIME, CALVIN.

WHERE'S HOBBES?

I SUPPOSE HE'S WHEREVER YOU LEFT HIM.

YOU MEAN HE'S STILL IN THE WOODS?! IT'S NIGHT OUT!

WHAT HAVE I TOLD YOU ABOUT LEAVING YOUR BELONGINGS?

HOBBES IS LOST! I'LL GET A FLASHLIGHT! WE'VE GOT TO FIND HIM!

HOBBES! HOBBES!

CALVIN, IT'S YOUR BEDTIME! DON'T YOU PULL THIS STUNT *NOW!*

CALVIN AND HOBBES by WATTERSON

HOBBES, YOU MANGY FUZZ-BRAINED LUNKHEAD, WHERE ARE YOU??

...I DIDN'T MEAN THAT QUITE THE WAY THAT SOUNDED.

C'MON, CALVIN, GET BACK INSIDE. IT'S TOO LATE TO GO SEARCHING FOR YOUR STUFFED TIGER NOW.

I CAN'T LEAVE HOBBES ALONE IN THE WOODS AT NIGHT!

WELL, MAYBE YOU SHOULD HAVE THOUGHT ABOUT THAT BEFORE IT GOT DARK. THIS CAN BE A LITTLE LESSON, HMM?

I THOUGHT HE'D COME BACK BY HIMSELF. I DIDN'T THINK HE'D GET LOST!

WE'LL LOOK FOR HIM TOMORROW. NOW OFF TO BED WITH YOU.

(SNIFF) I HOPE HE'S OK. IF HE HADN'T BEEN ACTING SO STUPID I NEVER WOULD'VE LEFT HIM.

I SURE WISH HE'D COME BACK.

CALVIN LEFT HOBBES SOMEWHERE IN THE WOODS. THE POOR KID'S PRETTY UPSET.

I'LL BET.

I MEAN, HE'S REALLY UPSET.

I SAID I'LL BET HE IS.

REALLY UPSET.

..AHH...

WOULD MY DAD HAVE DONE THIS? OF COURSE NOT. I WAS NEVER SPOILED LIKE THIS...

69

HI, CALVIN. I BROUGHT MR. BUN OVER SO WE CAN PLAY HOUSE. YOU AND I CAN BE THE PARENTS, AND HOBBES AND MR. BUN CAN BE OUR CHILDREN.

OH, RIGHT. HOBBES AND I ARE GONNA PUT OUR BIG PLANS ON HOLD SO WE CAN PLAY HOUSE WITH A STUFFED RABBIT? FORGET IT!

I DON'T SEE WHY YOU'LL PLAY WITH YOUR DUMB OL' TIGER AND NOT WITH MR. BUN AND ME! YOU'RE JUST MEAN, THAT'S ALL!

GO PLAY IN A MICROWAVE, SUSIE. WE'RE BUSY.

GIRLS ARE LIKE SLUGS— THEY PROBABLY SERVE SOME PURPOSE, BUT IT'S HARD TO IMAGINE WHAT.

MR. BUN SEEMS COMATOSE. DID YOU NOTICE?

HI, DAD. I'M REPEATING EVERYTHING ANYONE SAYS.

OH, YOU ARE, ARE YOU?

OH, YOU ARE, ARE YOU?

KNOCK IT OFF, CALVIN. THAT'S VERY ANNOYING.

KNOCK IT OFF, CALVIN. THAT'S VERY ANNOYING.

I FORFEIT ALL MY DESSERTS FOR A WEEK.

OK, GIVE THEM TO *ME*.

HA HA. WHY DON'T YOU GO BOTHER YOUR MOTHER FOR A WHILE?

WHERE ARE YOU GOING WITH THE TOY TELEPHONE?

OUT IN THE WOODS. YOU CAN COME ALONG IF YOU'D LIKE.

WHAT ARE YOU GOING TO DO?

TRY SOME BIRD CALLS.

Calvin and Hobbes by WATTERSON

UH OH, IT HAPPENED AGAIN.

CALVIN WAKES UP WITHOUT ANY RECOGNIZABLE FEATURES, SAVE TWO ANTENNAE. HOW DISGUSTING.

HE OOZES OUT OF BED ON A TRAIL OF SLIME. LACKING ARMS AND LEGS, HOW WILL CALVIN PUT ON HIS CLOTHES?

AREN'T YOU DRESSED YET? YOU ARE SO SLUGGISH IN THE MORNING!

PSST...SUSIE! WHAT'S THE ANSWER TO QUESTION FOUR?

IMADOOFUS.

THANKS!

THE TOOTH FAIRY'S GONNA MAKE YOU RICH TONIGHT, SUSIE.

LET'S SEE WHAT YOU DREW FOR ART CLASS, SUSIE.

WELL, A TIDY LITTLE DOMESTIC SCENE. A HOUSE IN A YARD WITH FLOWERS. HOW TYPICALLY FEMALE.

GIRLS THINK SMALL AND ARE PREOCCUPIED WITH PETTY DETAILS. BUT *BOYS* THINK *BIG!* BOYS THINK ABOUT ACTION AND ACCOMPLISHMENT! NO WONDER IT'S *MEN* WHO CHANGE THE WORLD!

YEAH? WHAT DID *YOU* DRAW?

A SQUADRON OF B-1s NUKING NEW YORK.

MOM, CAN HOBBES AND I RENT A VCR AND A TAPE TONIGHT?

I DON'T THINK SO, CALVIN. IT'S A SCHOOL NIGHT.

WHAT IF WE GOT AN *EDUCATIONAL* TAPE?

LIKE WHAT?

"CANNIBAL STEWARDESS VIXENS UNCHAINED."

NOW SHE WON'T EVEN LET US GO INTO THE *STORE*.

I THINK WE'D LEARN A *LOT* BY WATCHING THAT.

NOBODY HAD BETTER BE SNEAKING UP ON ME!!

WHUMP!

IT'S HARD TO CHANGE DIRECTION IN MID-AIR.

BUDDY, I'M GOING TO CHANGE A LOT MORE THAN YOUR DIRECTION.

SNIP SNAP CRACK

SHICKA SHICKA

WWHISSSHHH

F SHOOF SHOOF SHOOF SHO

KRITCH KRUNCH KRITCH KRUNCH

SOMETIMES IT'S GOOD TO HUSH UP A WHILE AND LET AUTUMN STICK IN A FEW WORDS.

CALVIN AND HOBBES by WATTERSON

A DAZED SPACEMAN SPIFF CRAWLS FROM THE SMOKING WRECKAGE OF HIS SHIP!

OUR HERO NOW REGRETS NOT BUYING A TOWING RIDER ON HIS INSURANCE POLICY.

THE COURAGEOUS SPACEMAN SPIFF HAS BEEN CAPTURED BY THE HIDEOUS ZORGS OF PLANET X-13!

LED THROUGH THE DANK CORRIDORS OF THE DUNGEON, SPIFF LOOKS IN VAIN FOR AN OPPORTUNITY TO ESCAPE!

OUR HERO IS BROUGHT BEFORE THE ZORG DESPOT!

SO *THIS* IS THE FAMED SPACE EXPLORER SPIFF! I'VE WAITED A LONG TIME FOR THIS MOMENT, EARTHLING SCUM!

YOU HAVE KNOWLEDGE WE NEED. COOPERATE, AND WE'LL KILL YOU RATHER PAINLESSLY.

LET'S DISPENSE WITH THE PLEASANTRIES, YOU TWISTED SPACE CRUSTACEAN. WHAT IS IT YOU WANT FROM ME?

A SUMMARY OF LEWIS AND CLARK'S EXPEDITION TO THE PACIFIC!

HA! WILD ZONTARS COULDN'T DRAG THAT INFORMATION OUT OF ME! DO YOUR WORST!

YOU DIDN'T READ THE ASSIGNMENT, DID YOU, CALVIN?

Hey, Calvin, c'mere.

SHOVE

Ha ha ha! What a weenie! Ha ha ha!

PEOPLE WHO GET NOSTALGIC ABOUT CHILDHOOD WERE OBVIOUSLY NEVER CHILDREN.

WATERSON

YOU LOOK DOWN IN THE DUMPS.

I AM.

MOE KEEPS KNOCKING ME DOWN AT SCHOOL FOR NO REASON. HE'S MEAN JUST FOR KICKS.

I SURE AM GLAD YOU'RE AN ANIMAL. ANIMALS SOMETIMES MAKE A LOT MORE SENSE THAN PEOPLE DO.

...AND WE'RE CUTER, TOO.

RIGHT, HOBBES. GOOD POINT.

WATERSON

LOOK, HOBBES, I NEED YOU TO COME TO SCHOOL WITH ME AND SHOW MOE A LITTLE FANG, OK?

YOU DON'T NEED TO KILL HIM OR ANYTHING. JUST GIVE 'IM SOMETHING TO THINK ABOUT ON THE WAY TO SURGERY.

HE USUALLY COMES AFTER ME AT RECESS, SO WE'LL GET HIM THEN. HEY, YOU DON'T HAVE RABIES, DO YOU?

CERTAINLY NOT.

RATS. WELL, I SUPPOSE HE'D AT LEAST HAVE TO GET A TETANUS SHOT.

WATERSON

Row 1

HEY, CALVIN, WHY'D YOU BRING YOUR STUFFED TIGER TO SCHOOL? IT'S NOT A SHOW AND TELL DAY.

I KNOW. HOBBES IS GOING TO GIVE MOE A LITTLE "TREAT" TODAY: A RIDE IN AN AMBULANCE HELICOPTER.

YEAH? HOW'S HE GOING TO DO *THAT*?

IF YOU HAVE AN AVERSION TO DESCRIPTIONS OF CARNAGE, YOU PROBABLY DON'T WANT TO KNOW.

TALKING WITH YOU IS SORT OF THE CONVERSATIONAL EQUIVALENT OF AN OUT-OF-BODY EXPERIENCE.

DON'T GET TOO CLOSE NOW. I WANT HOBBES TO STAY FRESH FOR THIS AFTERNOON.

Row 2

Look, Calvin's got a teddy bear. That's real sweet, Cal.

IT'S A TIGER, YOU BRAINLESS INVERTEBRATE.

Hey, maybe I'd like to play with your teddy!

GOOD IDEA, MOE. HOBBES PLAYS KINDA ROUGH, BUT HE'S *LOTS* OF FUN. C'MERE AND TAKE HIM.

Why? Is the teacher watching? This is a trick, right? I'm not touching your stupid teddy, see?

C'MON, I DARE YOU! WHAT'S THE MATTER? ARE YOU CHICKEN?

HA HA! BOY, YOU SURE SCARED *HIM* OFF! YOU WERE GREAT!

COME BACK AND CALL ME A "BEAR" AGAIN! YEAH, *YOU*, BUB!!

Row 3

I CALLED YOUR TEACHER ABOUT MOE'S BULLYING, AND SHE SAID SHE'D PUT A STOP TO IT.

I'M AFRAID YOU WASTED YOUR TIME, MOM. MOE TOOK ONE LOOK AT HOBBES AND JUST ABOUT LOST HIS LUNCH!

I DON'T THINK MOE WILL BE BOTHERING *ME* FOR A WHILE. IT'S NOT EVERY KID WHO HAS A *TIGER* FOR A BEST FRIEND.

...AND WHAT LUCKY MOMS THOSE OTHER KIDS HAVE.

C'MON, HOBBES, IF YOU'LL LEND ME A BUCK, I'LL BUY YOU A COMIC BOOK.

PROCESSED LUNCH MEAT IS PRETTY SCARY. WHAT **ARE** THESE LITTLE SPECKS, ANYWAY? LIZARD PARTS? WHO KNOWS?

AND THIS "SKIN". I HEARD IT USED TO BE MADE OF INTESTINE, BUT I THINK NOWADAYS IT'S PLASTIC.

OF COURSE, THEY DYE AND WAX FRUIT SO IT LOOKS BETTER. IT'S LIKE EATING A CANDLE.

AND MOM WONDERS WHY I'M SO HUNGRY AFTER SCHOOL.

YEP, WE'D PROBABLY BE DEAD NOW IF IT WASN'T FOR TWINKIES.

HEY, DAD, YOUR LATEST POLL JUST CAME IN. LET'S SEE WHAT IT SAYS.

BE STILL, MY HEART.

WELL, I'LL BE! YOUR POPULARITY IS IMPROVING! YOU WENT UP 30 POINTS!

REALLY?

HECK, NO WONDER! I'M READING THE GRAPH UPSIDE-DOWN. WHAT A KLUTZ I AM!

...HOPE YOU'RE ALL PACKED, DAD.

DON'T YOU HAVE SOME HOMEWORK TO DO?

SNIFF SNIFF

I LIKE TO MESS WITH HIS DREAMS.

ZZ...COOKIES? FOR ME? WHY SURE, BACK UP THE TRUCK... ZZZZ

BU-URRP!

GOOD HEAVENS, CALVIN! WHAT DO WE SAY AFTER THAT?

"MUST BE A BARGE COMING THROUGH!"

WHAT DO YOU SAY?!

"THAT SURE TASTED BETTER GOING DOWN THAN COMING UP!"

THREE STRIKES AND YOU'RE HISTORY, KIDDO.

EXCUSE ME.

WITH ULTRA-SONIC HEARING, STUPENDOUS MAN NOTICES A CRY OF DISTRESS FROM A DISTANT ALLEYWAY!

HE LEAPS TO THE EDGE OF THE BUILDING AND PREPARES TO SWOOP TO THE RESCUE!

STUPENDOUS MAN HAD NOT QUITE REALIZED JUST HOW HIGH UP HE WAS, HOWEVER. AT THIS ALTITUDE THE WINDS WERE A LITTLE TRICKY, AND...

ARE YOU GOING, OR DO YOU NEED A PUSH?

DON'T RUSH ME, ALL RIGHT?!

ACK! ICK!

ACKPT! GHK!

HA-HA-HA-HA BLECHTH GAKCK

LURCH YOUR WAY TO THE CAR, KID. YOU NEED A HAIRCUT.

CalViN and HobbeS

by WATERSON

YOUR DAD'S WORKING, SO TRY NOT TO BOTHER HIM, OK?

DAD, I HAVE A QUESTION.

YES?

DO PEOPLE EVER SPONTANEOUSLY COMBUST?

UH... NOT THAT I KNOW OF, NO.

THAT'S A RELIEF. THANKS, DAD.

YOU'RE WELCOME.

POW!

DID I FOOL YOU?

IF YOU'RE HAVING TROUBLE THINKING OF WAYS TO MAKE YOURSELF USEFUL, I'LL GIVE YOU SOME SUGGESTIONS.

THINK IT'S GETTING ANY COLDER OUT? NOT REALLY.

I DON'T THINK IT'S GONNA CHANGE. ME EITHER.

NUTS. WELL, LET'S GO IN.

WHATCHA DOIN'? COUNTERFEITING MONEY.

IT'S REALLY HARD. LOOK AT ALL THE LITTLE LINES ON THIS BILL.

THINK ANYONE WILL FALL FOR YOUR FORGERY? SURE. EVERYONE WILL.

OL' GEORGE HAS THE GOUT, I SEE. I *SAID* THIS WAS HARD.

THE GIANT WHALE SWIMS TOWARD THE SURFACE!

ITS MASSIVE TAIL PUMPING FURIOUSLY, HE GAINS TERRIFYING MOMENTUM!

THE 35-TON BEHEMOTH BREACHES! HE CRASHES INTO THE SURF WITH DEAFENING IMPACT!

CALVIN, YOU'D BETTER NOT BE SPLASHING THE FLOOR, YOU HEAR ME?!

STIR
STIR
STIR

STIR
STIR
STIR

I WON'T EAT ANY CEREAL THAT DOESN'T TURN THE MILK PURPLE.

THE DEADLY TORNADO MAKES ITS WAY ACROSS THE COMMUNITY!

THE CIRCLING UPDRAFT CLOCKS AT OVER 200 MPH! THE TWISTER SEARCHES FOR A TRAILER PARK!

FINDING ONE, IT TOUCHES DOWN! DEBRIS IS THROWN FOR MILES IN THE ENSUING EXPLOSION OF RUSHING AIR!

WHEN ARE YOU GOING TO CLEAN UP THIS ROOM?! IT LOOKS LIKE A...

TORNADO HIT IT, I KNOW.

OH BOY, IT'S SATURDAY!!

WHAT'S GOING ON? WHY AREN'T THERE ANY CARTOONS ON TV? IT'S JUST A TEST PATTERN.

THE TV GUIDE SAYS THEY DON'T START UNTIL 6:30.

HECK, THAT'S 45 MINUTES FROM NOW! WELL, C'MON, I'LL RACE YOU UP AND DOWN THE STAIRS!

WHY CAN'T HE EVER GET UP LIKE THIS ON SCHOOL DAYS?

GO BREAK HIS LITTLE LEGS, WILL YOU, HONEY?

BANG!
★
BONK
☆
⊙

BAD NEWS ON YOUR CAMPAIGN TO STAY DAD, DAD.

OH?

YEP. THE LATEST POLL OF SIX-YEAR-OLDS IN THIS HOUSEHOLD SHOWS THAT THEY DON'T CARE ABOUT ISSUES THIS YEAR. IT'S CHARACTER THAT COUNTS.

SO WHY IS THAT BAD NEWS?

WHO'S THE BIMBO WITH YOU IN THIS OLD PROM PICTURE?

THAT "BIMBO" IS YOUR MOTHER!

WHO'S A BIMBO?!

PRETTY FUNKY HAIRDO, MOM!

IT'S THE SAD TRUTH, DAD. NOBODY CARES ABOUT YOUR POSITIONS ON FATHERHOOD. WE JUST WANT TO KNOW ABOUT YOUR CHARACTER.

IF YOU'RE GOING TO BE DAD HERE, WE HAVE TO KNOW YOU'VE NEVER DONE OR SAID ANYTHING THAT WOULD REFLECT POORLY ON YOUR JUDGMENT.

I HAVE YOUR COLLEGE YEARBOOK HERE. LET'S FLIP THROUGH IT, SHALL WE?

IS THIS YOU WITH THE KEG AND THE "PARTY NAKED" T-SHIRT?

GIVE ME THAAAT!

GRANDPA SAYS THE COMICS WERE A LOT BETTER YEARS AGO WHEN NEWSPAPERS PRINTED THEM BIGGER.

HE SAYS COMICS NOW ARE JUST A BUNCH OF XEROXED TALKING HEADS BECAUSE THERE'S NO SPACE TO TELL A DECENT STORY OR TO SHOW ANY ACTION.

HE THINKS PEOPLE SHOULD WRITE TO THEIR NEWSPAPERS AND COMPLAIN.

YOUR GRANDPA TAKES THE FUNNIES PRETTY SERIOUSLY.

YEAH, MOM'S LOOKING INTO NURSING HOMES.

QUIT HOGGING THE BED. YOU'RE WAY OVER ON MY SIDE.

TOUGH BEANS, FUZZ FACE.

EVER THINK ABOUT GEYSERS AND WATERFALLS? HUNDREDS OF THOUSANDS OF GALLONS OF WATER! FLOWING, SPILLING, RUSHING, GUSHING, SPLASHING!

HE REALLY FIGHTS MEAN.

SPACEMAN SPIFF FLEES THE DESPICABLE SCUM BEINGS OF PLANET Q-13!

IN A SURPRISE MANEUVER, OUR HERO TURNS TO FACE THE ADVERSARY! HIS HAND TIGHTENS AROUND THE DEATH RAY TRIGGER!

IT DOESN'T RESPOND! SPIFF REACHES FOR THE MERTILIZER BEAM, BUT IT DOESN'T WORK EITHER! NEITHER DO THE PHOSPHO BOMBS OR THE MORDO BLASTERS! NOTHING IS WORKING!!

1812! GETTYSBURG! 16 FLUID OUNCES! I BEFORE E! THOMAS EDISON!

PERHAPS SOMEONE WHO HAS BEEN *PAYING ATTENTION* CAN HELP OUT CALVIN?

Z

YAAHH!

I KEEP FORGETTING THAT FIVE OF HIS SIX ENDS ARE POINTY WHEN HE LIES LIKE THAT.

SINCE SEPTEMBER, IT'S JUST GOTTEN COLDER AND COLDER.

THERE'S LESS DAYLIGHT NOW, I'VE NOTICED, TOO.

OH NO! THIS CAN ONLY MEAN ONE THING!

THE SUN IS GOING OUT! IN A FEW MORE MONTHS EARTH WILL BE A DARK AND LIFELESS BALL OF ICE!

WELL, GEE, NOW I DON'T FEEL SO BAD ABOUT NOT SETTING UP AN IRA LAST YEAR.

DAD SAYS THE SUN ISN'T GOING OUT.

HE SAYS IT'S COLDER BECAUSE OUR HEMISPHERE IS TILTED AWAY FROM THE SUN NOW.

HE SAYS WINTER WILL BE HERE SOON.

ISN'T IT SAD HOW SOME PEOPLE'S GRIP ON THEIR LIVES IS SO PRECARIOUS THAT THEY'LL EMBRACE ANY PREPOSTEROUS DELUSION RATHER THAN FACE AN OCCASIONAL BLEAK TRUTH?

ARE YOU GOING TO LIVE THE LAST FEW MONTHS OF YOUR LIFE ANY DIFFERENTLY, NOW THAT THE SUN IS GOING OUT AND WE'RE ALL DOOMED?

NO, I'VE ALWAYS BELIEVED IN LIVING EACH DAY AS IF IT WAS MY LAST, SO I NEVER HAVE ANY REGRETS.

KIND OF INSPIRING, HUH?

IF YOU WERE SOMEONE ELSE, IT MIGHT BE.

PASS ME THAT ISSUE OF CAPTAIN NAPALM WILL YOU?

MY TEACHER SAID THE SAME THING DAD DID. THE SUN *ISN'T* GOING OUT AFTER ALL!

IT'S JUST GETTING COLDER BECAUSE WINTER'S COMING. DAD WAS RIGHT ALL ALONG!

IMAGINE OL' DAD KNOWING SOMETHING LIKE THAT!

WHAT'S THIS STORY YOU'RE GOING TO READ ME, DAD? IT DOESN'T HAVE ANY ROMANCE IN IT, DOES IT?

UH...

EDIT IT OUT IF IT DOES. I HATE ROMANCE. DOES IT HAVE ANY BORING DESCRIPTION IN IT?

WELL...

SKIP IT IF YOU SEE ANY. I LIKE MY STORIES FAST AND GRIPPING.

IT DOESN'T HAVE A MORAL, DOES IT? I HATE BEING TOLD HOW TO LIVE MY LIFE. SKIP THE MORAL, TOO, OK?

DOES HIS MAJESTY PREFER COLOR PICTURES, OR BLACK AND WHITE?

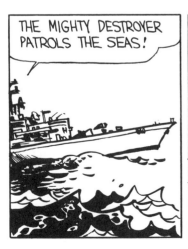

THE MIGHTY DESTROYER PATROLS THE SEAS!

SUDDENLY THE SHIP SPINS OUT OF CONTROL! IT'S CAUGHT IN A WHIRLPOOL!

WITHIN MOMENTS THE GIANT VESSEL DIPS ITS HULL INTO THE SWIRLING VORTEX AND IS NEVER SEEN AGAIN!

OH NO! HERE GOES THE REST OF THE NAVY!

ARE YOU LETTING *THE WATER OUT ALREADY?*

CALVIN and HOBBES
by WATTERSON

ZZ-ZZZZ

BBWAAHHH

CALVIN, IT'S TIME TO WAKE UP.

Z

CALVIN, IT'S TIME TO WAKE UP.

C'MON, YOU'LL BE LATE FOR SCHOOL.

Z

MY DREAMS ARE GETTING WAY TOO LITERAL.

I ALWAYS WANTED TO BE A CUB SCOUT AND GET MERIT BADGES AND STUFF, BUT I HATE GOING TO MEETINGS.

OK OK, JUST READ ABOUT KNOTS, ALL RIGHT?

HEY, LOOK, HERE'S A MOTTO! I DIDN'T KNOW YOU HAD A MOTTO! WOW, WHAT FUN!

"LIVE FOR REVENGE" IS GOING TO BE MY MOTTO IF YOU DON'T GET ME OUT OF THIS.

WATERSON

I'LL QUIZ YOU. WHAT DO YOU DO FOR A SECOND-DEGREE BURN?

DON'T FLIP THROUGH THE BOOK, YOU IDIOT! UNTIE ME!

HMPH, IF I WAS IN YOUR PREDICAMENT, I'D TREAT ME WITH A LOT MORE RESPECT. DO YOU SAY YOU'RE SORRY?

MMFF! RRGGH! OOH! ARGH! YOU DIRTY ROTTEN STINKING

HOBBES, I'M NOT KIDDING. IF YOU DON'T GET ME LOOSE IN TEN SECONDS...

YOU GOT YOUR-SELF INTO THIS, "MR. HOUDINI," NOT ME.

BUT I'M SUPPOSED TO BE AT DINNER! MOM'S GONNA KILL ME!

ESCAPE ARTISTS HAVE A RISKY TRADE. HEY, HERE'S MORSE CODE!

OK, I'M SORRY I CALLED YOU NAMES. I SAID I'M SORRY, RIGHT? NOW UNTIE ME!

HERE'S HOW YOU SAY "BANANA" IN MORSE. DASH DOT DOT DOT, DOT DASH...

WATERSON

WHAT IS THAT KID DOING?! IT SOUNDS LIKE A CHAIR THUMPING AROUND THE ROOM.

BONK BONK

WELL, HIS DINNER IS STONE COLD. I HOPE HE'S HAPPY.

ALL RIGHT, YOUNG MAN! YOU'VE WASTED THE NICE MEAL YOUR MOM FIXED. GET OUT HERE.

WATERSON

YOU TIED YOURSELF UP?? WHAT ON EARTH WERE YOU DOING?!

HOBBES TIED ME UP, DAD! IT'S HIS FAULT!

DON'T MAKE UP LIES, CALVIN. HOW DID YOU GET YOURSELF LIKE THIS?!

HOBBES DID IT, DAD! HE WAS GOING TO HOLD ME FOR RANSOM! HONEST!

RANSOM?? WHO'D PAY FOR YOU, YOU BIG FIBBER?! I'M CERTAINLY GLAD YOUR DAD SAW THROUGH THAT FILTHY LIE!

OH, HUSH. YOU ALWAYS GET ME IN TROUBLE.

CALVIN and HOBBES by WATTERSON

First there was nothing...

...then there was Calvin!

Calvin, the mighty god, creates the universe with pure will!

From utter nothingness comes swirling form! Life begins where once was void!

But Calvin is no kind and loving god! He's one of the old gods! He demands sacrifice!

Yes, Calvin is a god of the underworld! And the puny inhabitants of earth displease him!

The great Calvin ignores their pleas for mercy and the doomed writhe in agony!

HAVE YOU SEEN HOW ABSORBED CALVIN IS WITH THOSE TINKERTOYS? HE'S CREATING WHOLE WORLDS OVER THERE!

I'LL BET HE GROWS UP TO BE AN ARCHITECT.

99

AH.. **AH**.. **AH**..

*

I JUTH **HADE** IT WHED THITH HAPPEDTH.

CALVIN THE CRIMINAL IS ABOUT TO FACE JUSTICE! ANGRY THRONGS TURN OUT TO WATCH HIS EXECUTION!

AS HE IS LED UP THE GALLOWS, HE REFLECTS UPON HIS MANY HEINOUS CRIMES. HE IS NOT REPENTANT!

THE NOOSE IS PUT AROUND HIS NECK AND TIGHTENED! THIS IS THE END!

GACKK URRGHH

OH, KNOCK IT OFF. SOME OF US HAVE TO WEAR A TIE EVERY DAY.

HOW WAS THE KIDDY MATINEE MOVIE?

MOVIE? OH, YEAH, THE MOVIE. YEAH, THERE WAS A MOVIE. IT WAS OK, I GUESS.

HOW WAS THE MATINEE?

WE... ARE... BUYING... A VIDEO PLAYER.

Calvin and Hobbes

by WATTERSON

YAWN

SCRITCH SCRATCH

RUB RUB RUB

SHOOF SHOOF SHOOF

ITCH ITCH ITCH ITCH

HMMMMM

THAT SIGH OUGHT TO GET ME OUT OF A FEW YEARS' PURGATORY.

Calvin and Hobbes

by WATTERSON

CAN WE GET *THIS* TREE, MOM? CAN WE?

I DON'T KNOW, CALVIN. IT'S AWFULLY EXPENSIVE.

YEAH, BUT JUST THINK HOW MUCH LOOT WOULD FIT UNDER IT!

DAD! COME BRING IN THE CHRISTMAS TREE MOM AND I PICKED! IT'S A GREAT ONE!

THIS YEAR I THOUGHT WE'D JUST KEEP THE TREE IN THE GARAGE.

IN THE GARAGE?!

SURE. YOU CAN GO OUT AND LOOK AT IT ANY TIME YOU LIKE, AND IT SAVES ALL THE TROUBLE OF DECORATING IT.

WE'RE NOT GOING TO DECORATE IT?!?

WHY BOTHER? WE JUST TAKE IT ALL DOWN IN TWO WEEKS. ON CHRISTMAS DAY, IF YOU GET A PRESENT...

IF I GET A PRESENT?!

...YOU CAN TAKE IT OUT TO THE GARAGE TO OPEN, AND PRETEND THE TREE HAS LOTS OF LIGHTS, AND...

MOMMMM!

I KNOW SOMEBODY WHO'S GOING TO GET A LOT OF COAL IN HIS STOCKING, BUSTER.

THIS SEASON GETS LESS JOLLY EVERY YEAR.

Dear Santa,

Attached is my Christmas list for this year.

Last year I did not receive several items from my list.

For your convenience, I have grouped those items together on page 12. Please check them carefully, and include them with the rest of my loot this year.

THAT'S THE PROBLEM WITH THIS GUY. HE'S GOTTEN SLOPPY WITHOUT ANY COMPETITION.

HE SEES YOU WHEN YOU'RE SLEEPING, HE KNOWS WHEN YOU'RE AWAKE...

HE KNOWS IF YOU'VE BEEN BAD OR GOOD, SO BE GOOD FOR GOODNESS SAKE!

* CLICK *

SANTA CLAUS: KINDLY OLD ELF, OR CIA SPOOK?

THIS SANTA CLAUS STUFF BOTHERS ME.... ESPECIALLY THE JUDGE AND JURY BIT.

WHO APPOINTED SANTA? HOW DO WE KNOW HE'S IMPARTIAL? WHAT CRITERIA DOES HE USE FOR DETERMINING GOOD AND BAD?

AND WHAT ABOUT EXTENUATING CIRCUMSTANCES? KIDS SHOULD HAVE THE BENEFIT OF LEGAL COUNSEL, DON'T YOU THINK?

YOU'RE WORRIED ABOUT THE SALAMANDER INCIDENT, AREN'T YOU?

TEMPORARY INSANITY! THAT'S ALL IT WAS!

THEY SAY SANTA KNOWS IF YOU'VE BEEN GOOD OR BAD, BUT WHAT IF SOMEONE HAD BEEN SORT OF *BOTH*?

I MEAN, SUPPOSE SOME KID *TRIED* TO BE GOOD... AT LEAST, WELL, MOST OF THE TIME... BUT BAD THINGS INEXPLICABLY KEPT HAPPENING?

SUPPOSE SOME KID JUST HAD TERRIBLE LUCK, AND HE GOT BLAMED FOR A LOT OF THINGS HE DID ONLY *SORT* OF ON PURPOSE?

WHO EXACTLY MIGHT WE BE TALKING ABOUT?

THIS IS A PURELY HYPOTHETICAL CASE, MR. SMARTY PANTS.

THIS WHOLE SANTA CLAUS THING JUST DOESN'T MAKE SENSE.

WHY ALL THE SECRECY? WHY ALL THE MYSTERY? IF THE GUY EXISTS, WHY DOESN'T HE EVER SHOW HIMSELF AND PROVE IT?

AND IF HE *DOESN'T* EXIST, WHAT'S THE MEANING OF ALL THIS?

I DUNNO... ISN'T THIS A RELIGIOUS HOLIDAY?

YEAH, BUT ACTUALLY, I'VE GOT THE SAME QUESTIONS ABOUT GOD.

GOSH, HOBBES, WHAT IF I DON'T GET ANY PRESENTS THIS YEAR BECAUSE I DOUBTED THE EXISTENCE OF SANTA?

SUPPOSE HE'S PUTTING MY NAME ON THE "BAD" LIST RIGHT NOW! THAT WOULD BE AWFUL!

PERSONALLY, I'D THINK THAT IF YOU WEREN'T ON THE "BAD" LIST ALL ALONG, THIS WOULDN'T PUSH YOU OVER.

THANKS FOR THE COMFORT, EGGNOG BRAIN.

SEE? *SEE* WHY YOU'RE ON THE "BAD" LIST? INSULTS!

WELL, I'VE DECIDED I *DO* BELIEVE IN SANTA CLAUS, NO MATTER HOW PREPOSTEROUS HE SOUNDS.

WHAT CONVINCED YOU?

A SIMPLE RISK ANALYSIS.

I WANT PRESENTS. *LOTS* OF PRESENTS. WHY RISK NOT GETTING THEM OVER A MATTER OF BELIEF? HECK, I'LL BELIEVE ANYTHING THEY WANT.

HOW CYNICALLY ENTERPRISING OF YOU.

IT'S THE SPIRIT OF CHRISTMAS.

PSST! ARE YOU AWAKE?

OF COURSE.

I HAVEN'T HEARD SANTA YET, HAVE YOU? DO YOU THINK HE'S COMING?

IT'S ONLY 11:00. WE MAY BE LATER ON THE ROUTE.

THUMP!

* GASP * DID YOU HEAR THAT?

IT'S HIM! IT'S SANTA! SHHH! HE'S SAYING SOMETHING!

SLIPPIN' RIPPIN' DANG FANG ROTTEN ZARG BARG-A-DING DONG!

QUIET, DEAR! CALVIN WILL HEAR YOU!

WE GOT PRESENTS! SANTA CAME! HE CAME! HE CAME!

OH, NO... IT'S NOT MORNING ALREADY?

WELL, TECHNICALLY, YES...

WHAT DO YOU THINK IS THE MEANING OF TRUE HAPPINESS?

IS IT MONEY, CARS AND WOMEN?

..OR IS IT JUST MONEY AND CARS?

WELL-L-L-L?

LOOK AT THIS! YOU CALL THIS SNOW?!

IT'S NOT EVEN AN INCH HIGH! WHAT GOOD IS LESS THAN AN INCH OF SNOW?!

WELL, IT'S PRETTY.

NOBODY EVER CLOSED A SCHOOL ON ACCOUNT OF PRETTINESS.

THIS WILL BE THE STRONGEST SNOW FORT EVER MADE!

KEEP PACKING ON SNOW. THIS WILL BE INDESTRUCTIBLE.

WE'LL POUR WATER ON IT, SO IT FREEZES OVERNIGHT. THAT WAY OUR FORT WILL BE HERE UNTIL JULY!

WHERE'S THAT KID?!

I HATE WAITING FOR THE SCHOOL BUS ON DAYS LIKE THESE.

BLUSTERY COLD DAYS SHOULD BE SPENT PROPPED UP IN BED WITH A MUG OF HOT CHOCOLATE AND A PILE OF COMIC BOOKS.

THAT'S WHAT I'D LIKE TO BE DOING RIGHT NOW.

AS SOON AS I GRADUATE, I'M GOING TO SPEND *EVERY* WINTER THAT WAY.

I WISH YOUR BUS WOULD COME. MY HOT CHOCOLATE WILL GET COLD.

HELP ME FIGURE OUT THIS HOMEWORK PROBLEM, HOBBES. WHAT'S 3 + 8 ?

OK, ASSIGN THE ANSWER A VALUE OF "X". "X" ALWAYS MEANS MULTIPLY, SO TAKE THE NUMERATOR (THAT'S LATIN FOR "NUMBER EIGHTER") AND PUT THAT ON THE OTHER SIDE OF THE EQUATION.

THAT LEAVES YOU WITH THREE ON THIS SIDE, SO WHAT TIMES THREE EQUALS EIGHT? THE ANSWER, OF COURSE, IS SIX.

GOSH, I MUST HAVE DONE ALL THE OTHERS WRONG.

THESE PROBLEMS SEEM AWFULLY ADVANCED FOR FIRST GRADE, IF YOU ASK ME.

HERE'S ANOTHER MATH PROBLEM I CAN'T FIGURE OUT. WHAT'S 9 + 4 ?

OOH, THAT'S A TRICKY ONE. YOU HAVE TO USE CALCULUS AND IMAGINARY NUMBERS FOR THIS.

IMAGINARY NUMBERS?!

YOU KNOW, ELEVENTEEN, THIRTY-TWELVE, AND ALL THOSE. IT'S A LITTLE CONFUSING AT FIRST.

HOW DID *YOU* LEARN ALL THIS? YOU'VE NEVER EVEN GONE TO SCHOOL!

INSTINCT. TIGERS ARE BORN WITH IT.

IT'S FREEZING IN THIS HOUSE! SOMEBODY CRANK UP THE THERMOSTAT! WHY DOESN'T SOMEONE MAKE A FIRE?!

IF WE CAN'T AFFORD TO HEAT THIS PLACE, MAYBE DAD SHOULD GET A BETTER JOB! WHY CAN'T WE MOVE TO FLORIDA?!

CALVIN, PIPE DOWN AND PUT ON A SWEATER IF YOU'RE COLD.

AND GO TO ALL THAT TROUBLE?!

I READ THAT THE AVERAGE HOUSEHOLD WATCHES 7½ HOURS OF TV EVERY DAY.

MOM SAYS SHE DOESN'T WATCH TV AT ALL WHILE I'M AT SCHOOL...

...SO IF I GET HOME AT 3:00, I SHOULD BE ABLE TO WATCH IT STRAIGHT TILL 10:30, RIGHT?

WRONG.

DO YOU WANT US TO BE SUB-AVERAGE?!

MOM, THE WASHER IS DONE.

OK.

AREN'T YOU GOING TO PUT THE WASH IN THE DRYER?

IN A MINUTE.

YOU MEAN YOU'RE JUST GOING TO LET IT SIT IN THE WASHING MACHINE?!?

CALVIN, CAN'T YOU SEE I'M BUSY RIGHT NOW??

SHE SAYS SHE'S BUSY.

I HOPE THE NEXT TIME SHE TAKES A BATH THERE AREN'T ANY TOWELS.

Calvin and Hobbes

by WATTERSON

WATTERSON

114

Calvin: WHO'S COMING TO VISIT?

Mom: YOUR UNCLE MAX. I THOUGHT I TOLD YOU.

Calvin: UNCLE MAX?? *I* DON'T REMEMBER ANY UNCLE MAX. ARE YOU SURE HE'S RELATED? MAYBE HE'S A CON MAN TRYING TO SWINDLE US!

Mom: OF COURSE HE'S RELATED. HE'S YOUR DAD'S BROTHER. HE JUST HASN'T BEEN HERE FOR A FEW YEARS.

Calvin: WHY NOT? WAS HE IN JAIL?

Mom: NO! GOOD HEAVENS, CALVIN.

Dad: NOW, NOW... WITH MAX, THAT'S NOT A BAD GUESS.

Dad: WE'RE GETTING NEAR THE AIRPORT, CALVIN. SEE THE JETS?

Dad: HOW COME YOU'RE SO QUIET BACK THERE? AREN'T YOU EXCITED TO SEE UNCLE MAX?

Calvin: ...YEAH...

Calvin: I JUST HOPE NOBODY THINKS I'M GIVING UP *MY* ROOM WHILE HE'S HERE.

Dad: IT'S GREAT TO SEE YOU, MAX! IT SEEMS LIKE AGES SINCE YOU'VE BEEN HERE.

Max: I'LL SAY.

Max: I DIDN'T THINK IT HAD BEEN SO LONG, UNTIL I SAW CALVIN. THIS GUY HAS REALLY GROWN.

Max: SO KID, WHAT DO YOU SAY?

Calvin: I SAY YOU'D BETTER WATCH YOUR STEP, 'CAUSE I'VE GOT A LIVE, MAN-EATING TIGER AT HOME, AND IF I SO MUCH AS WINK, HE'LL RIP YOUR LUNGS OUT.

Max: CUTE KID, BRO.

DO YOU HAVE ANY KIDS, UNCLE MAX?

ME? NOPE, I'M NOT EVEN MARRIED.

OH.

...WHAT DIFFERENCE DOES *THAT* MAKE?

KID WATCHES A LOT OF TV, DOES HE?

BOY, CALVIN TAKES THAT STUFFED TIGER EVERYWHERE HE GOES.

YEAH, THEY'RE INSEPARABLE.

DO YOU WORRY ABOUT THAT? I MEAN, SHOULDN'T HE BE PLAYING WITH REAL FRIENDS?

OH, I THINK HE WILL WHEN HE'S READY. DIDN'T YOU EVER HAVE AN IMAGINARY FRIEND?

SOMETIMES I THINK *ALL* MY FRIENDS HAVE BEEN IMAGINARY.

UNCLE MAX, LOOK! I'LL SHOW YOU A MAGIC DISAPPEARING TRICK!

OK, FIRST I'LL NEED AN ORDINARY TWENTY-DOLLAR BILL.

HOW ABOUT IF I LEND YOU A NICKEL INSTEAD?

NO, IT WORKS MUCH BETTER WITH A TWENTY. ...OR A FIFTY, IF YOU HAVE ONE.

I TAKE IT YOU THINK YOUR OL' UNCLE MAX IS A LOW-WATT BULB.

WHY, DID DAD TELL YOU HOW THIS WORKS?

AAGHH, I CAN'T BELIEVE WE WERE ASSIGNED TO DO A REPORT TOGETHER.

ALL I CAN SAY IS YOU'D BETTER DO A GREAT JOB! I DON'T WANT TO FLUNK JUST BECAUSE I WAS ASSIGNED A DOOFUS FOR A PARTNER.

A DOOFUS ?!? WHO TAKES HER SANDWICHES APART AND EATS EACH INGREDIENT SEPARATELY?

WHAT'S WRONG WITH THAT ?!

IT CERTIFIES YOU AS A GRADE "A" NIMROD.

IT DOES NOT!

OK, LOOK. WE'VE GOT TO DO THIS DUMB PROJECT TOGETHER, SO WE MIGHT AS WELL GET IT OVER WITH. WHAT ARE WE SUPPOSED TO BE DOING?

WEREN'T YOU EVEN PAYING ATTENTION ?! WHAT WOULD YOU DO IF I WASN'T HERE TO ASK ?? YOU'D FLUNK AND BE SENT BACK TO KINDERGARTEN, THAT'S WHAT!

SAYS YOU! I HEARD THAT SOMETIMES KIDS DON'T PAY ATTENTION BECAUSE THE CLASS GOES AT TOO SLOW OF A PACE FOR THEM. SOME OF US ARE TOO SMART FOR THE CLASS.

OH, RIGHT. YOU'RE TOO SMART.

BELIEVE IT, LADY. YOU KNOW HOW EINSTEIN GOT BAD GRADES AS A KID? WELL, MINE ARE EVEN WORSE!

SO WHAT ARE WE SUPPOSED TO BE DOING?

WE'RE SUPPOSED TO BE RESEARCHING THE PLANET MERCURY.

SO WHAT HAVE WE FOUND OUT?

NOTHING! I'M NOT GOING TO DO THIS WHOLE THING MYSELF!

YOU'D PROBABLY GOOF IT ALL UP IF YOU DID. LET'S GET STARTED.

YES! LET'S!

I'LL BE THE MANAGEMENT, AND YOU CAN BE THE LABOR. FIRST, GET SOME BOOKS.

DOES ANYONE WANT TO TRADE PARTNERS?

WE HAVE TO GIVE OUR REPORT ON PLANET MERCURY TODAY. DID YOU DO YOUR HALF?

OF COURSE I DID. AND I'LL BET MY HALF MAKES YOUR HALF LOOK PATHETIC.

IT HAD *BETTER* BE GOOD... OR ELSE!

THE PLANET MERCURY
An Exhaustively Researched Report by Calvin

WATERSON

",AND SO, THE PLANET MERCURY IS A HOT AND BARREN WORLD, THE CLOSEST TO OUR SUN."

AND TO TELL US ABOUT THE MYTHOLOGY OF MERCURY, HERE'S MY PARTNER, CALVIN.

THANK YOU, THANK YOU! HEY, WHAT A CROWD! YOU LOOK GREAT THIS MORNING...REALLY, I MEAN THAT! GO ON, GIVE YOURSELVES A HAND!

WATERSON

YOU KNOW, A FUNNY THING HAPPENED ON THE WAY TO THE LIBRARY YESTERDAY...

THIS ISN'T MY FAULT, MISS WORMWOOD!

THE PLANET MERCURY WAS NAMED AFTER A ROMAN GOD WITH WINGED FEET.

MERCURY WAS THE GOD OF FLOWERS AND BOUQUETS, WHICH IS WHY TODAY HE IS A REGISTERED TRADEMARK OF FTD FLORISTS.

WHY THEY NAMED A PLANET AFTER THIS GUY, I CAN'T IMAGINE.

...UM... BACK TO YOU, SUSIE.

WATERSON

BOY, YOU SHOULD'VE SEEN THE SPARKS FLY WHEN I GAVE MY HALF OF THE REPORT.

I'VE NEVER SEEN SUSIE SO MAD. SHE ACCUSED ME OF NOT DOING ANY RESEARCH AND CLAIMED I MADE UP THE WHOLE THING.

DID YOU?

HECK, NO. I JUST TOOK A FEW CREATIVE LIBERTIES.

AND THEY CALLED YOUR MOM OVER A FEW CREATIVE LIBERTIES?

GEEZ, YOU THINK *SUSIE* WAS MAD...

DON'T YOU HATE IT WHEN YOUR BOOGERS FREEZE?

HERE WE ARE, OVERLOOKING SUICIDE GULCH, ABOUT TO HURL OURSELVES DOWN AT BREAKNECK SPEED IN A SLED THAT HARDLY STEERS!

RISKING LIFE AND LIMB! LOOKING DEATH STRAIGHT IN THE EYE!

"WHY?" YOU ASK! WHY DO WE DO IT ??

BECAUSE WE GET PAID, I HOPE.

BECAUSE IT'S THERE!

CALVIN AND HOBBES
by WATTERSON

PLANET BOG— POOLS OF TOXIC CHEMICALS BUBBLE UNDER A CHOKING ATMOSPHERE OF POISONOUS GASES.

...BUT, ASIDE FROM THAT, IT'S NOT MUCH LIKE EARTH.

WE FIND SPACEMAN SPIFF STRUGGLING ACROSS THE TERRAIN OF A DISTANT PLANET!

SUDDENLY THE GROUND BEGINS TO SHAKE! A CLOUD OF DUST APPEARS ON THE HORIZON! IT'S A ZORG!!

OUR HERO RUNS FOR COVER, BUT THE ZORG IS INSTANTLY UPON HIM!

SPIFF FIRES HIS BLASTER, BUT THE WEAPON IS USELESS AGAINST THE MONSTER!

THE FEARLESS SPACE EXPLORER IS TAKEN TO THE ZORG'S CAVE, WHERE HE DISCOVERS A VAT OF BOILING WATER! OH NO! OUR HERO IS ABOUT TO BE COOKED ALIVE!

SPIFF'S MIND RACES FURIOUSLY...

WELL? GET IN.

DON'T YOU WANT TO LEAN WAY, WAY OVER, AND TEST HOW HOT THE WATER IS?

LOOK, HOBBES, THE LATEST PERFECTION IN TECHNOLOGY.

A WATER PISTOL?

HECK, NO! THIS IS THE NEW, IMPROVED VERSION OF THE TRANSMOGRIFIER.

NOW YOU CAN TRANSMOGRIFY THINGS JUST BY POINTING AT THEM! SAY YOU DON'T LIKE THE COLOR OF YOUR BEDSPREAD. WELL, YOU JUST ZAP IT, AND PRESTO, IT'S AN IGUANA!

ONE CAN CERTAINLY IMAGINE THE MYRIAD OF USES FOR A HAND-HELD IGUANA MAKER.

IT DOESN'T *HAVE* TO BE AN IGUANA. IT CAN BE ANYTHING. SUPPOSE MOM'S GETTING ON OUR NERVES, FOR INSTANCE...

HOW DOES THIS TRANSMOGRIFIER GUN KNOW WHAT TO TRANSMOGRIFY SOMETHING INTO?

TELEPATHY.

THE GUN AUTOMATICALLY READS THE BRAIN WAVES YOU EMIT, AND TURNS THE OBJECT INTO WHATEVER YOU WANT.

THAT'S AMAZING.

WELL, IT TOOK ME ALL MORNING TO INVENT.

SO SAY I'M THINKING ABOUT A BIG SLAB OF GRILLED TUNA NOW...

WATCH WHERE YOU'RE POINTING THAT! WATCH WHERE YOU'RE POINTING THAT!

OK, LET'S TEST THIS TRANSMOGRIFIER GUN.

I WANT TO BE A PTERODACTYL, SO YOU THINK OF ONE AND POINT THE TRANSMOGRIFIER AT ME.

THIS WILL BE GREAT. I'LL TERRORIZE THE NEIGHBORHOOD AWHILE AND THEN YOU CAN TRANSMOGRIFY ME BACK TO A BOY WHEN THE NATIONAL GUARD COMES.

WHAT'S A PTERODACTYL? SOME KIND OF BUG?

NO NO! IT'S A BIG FLYING DINOSAUR! DON'T SHOOT IF YOU DON'T KNOW WHAT IT IS!!

CALVIN and HOBBES

by WATTERSON

130

WHAT AM I GOING TO DO, HOBBES? I CAN'T BE AN OWL FOREVER!

HOW AM I GOING TO TRANSMOGRIFY BACK INTO A KID WHEN THE TRANSMOGRIFIER IS BROKEN?

MAYBE YOU SHOULD JUST LEARN TO ACCEPT THIS PREDICAMENT. IT'S NOT SO BAD BEING AN OWL INSTEAD OF A KID. ACTUALLY, IT'S PROBABLY BETTER.

BETTER?! HOW?

WELL, I NEVER QUITE KNEW HOW TO SAY THIS BEFORE, BUT LITTLE BOYS DON'T SMELL SO GOOD.

I'VE GOT TO GO TO SCHOOL TOMORROW MORNING! WHAT WILL THE KIDS SAY IF I'M AN OWL?!

OH, NO, I'M DOOMED! I'M DOOMED!

SINCE WHEN DO OWLS GO TO SCHOOL?

ZIP-A-DEE-DOO-DAH ZIP-A-DEE-AY! MY OH MY, WHAT A WONDERFUL DAY!

TIME TO GET UP, CALVIN. YOU DON'T WANT TO MISS THE SCHOOL BUS.

I'M NOT GOING TO SCHOOL, MOM. I'M AN OWL.

NO, YOU'RE NOT. NOW GET UP AND GET DRESSED.

I'M NOT AN OWL?

I'M NOT! I'M ME AGAIN! THE TRANSMOGRIFICATION MUST ONLY BE TEMPORARY! IT WORE OFF OVERNIGHT! I'M A KID! I CAN...

...GO...TO... SCHOOL.

.YAWWWNN.. KEEP THE SHADE DOWN WHEN YOU GO, OK?

COME IN, ROSALYN! I'M SORRY! WE DIDN'T REALIZE CALVIN HADN'T LET YOU IN.

THAT'S OK. IT WASN'T *TOO* COLD AND WET OUT.

WE'RE LATE. HELP YOURSELF TO ANYTHING IN THE FRIDGE. WE'LL SEE YOU AT TEN.

THE DOOR WAS JAMMED. REALLY. I COULDN'T GET IT OPEN.

BED.

HEY, DON'T FIX *THAT* FOR DINNER! DIDN'T MOM TELL YOU HOBBES AND I ARE ON A STRICT BIG MAC DIET? IT'S DOCTOR'S ORDERS!

OH, I'D BETTER CALL YOUR DOCTOR THEN!

OH, NO, SHE CALLED MY BLUFF! THE DOCTOR'S GONNA BE FURIOUS! BOY, ARE WE GOING TO GET IT!

I'M DIALING!

"WE"?

HELLO, DOCTOR? I'M CALLING ABOUT CALVIN'S DIETARY NEEDS.

..AT THE TONE, THE TIME WILL BE 6:27 AND 10 SECONDS. *BEEP*

BAD NEWS, CALVIN. YOUR DOCTOR SAYS YOU SHOULD HAVE A SPOONFUL OF CASTOR OIL AND LIE DOWN ALL EVENING.

HE DID? REALLY? NO, HE DIDN'T. DID HE? WHAT'S CASTOR OIL?

MOM DOESN'T SET THE TABLE THIS WAY. MOM DOES IT A LOT BETTER.

THIS FOOD SMELLS FUNNY. THIS ISN'T THE WAY MOM FIXES IT. I LIKE IT THE WAY MOM DOES IT BETTER.

I'M NOT YOUR MOM, ALL RIGHT?!

NO KIDDING! MY MOM LOVES ME MORE THAN LIFE ITSELF, AND SHE LETS ME DO ANYTHING I WANT. NOT LIKE *YOU*, YOU NASTY OL' BARRACUDA.

I CAN'T BELIEVE I POSTPONED A DATE FOR THIS.

Hey, Calvin, guess what we're doing in gym today. We're wrestling!

Next period you'll be so covered with mat burns you'll need skin grafts! Ha ha ha! See ya then, twinky.

SIGHHHHH...

PHYSICAL EDUCATION IS WHAT YOU LEARN FROM HAVING YOUR FACE IN SOMEONE'S ARMPIT RIGHT BEFORE LUNCH.

KAPWIINGGG! IT'S CALVIN, THE HUMAN LIGHT PARTICLE!

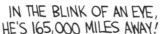

IN THE BLINK OF AN EYE, HE'S 165,000 MILES AWAY!

NOTHING IN THE UNIVERSE IS FASTER THAN CALVIN!

...I HOPE!

MUCH AS I LOVE MY "CHOCOLATE FROSTED CRUNCHY SUGAR BOMBS," THE BEST PART IS AFTER THE CEREAL IS GONE.

THAT'S WHEN YOU EAT THE LEFTOVER MILK THAT'S ALL SLUDGY FROM THE EXTRA SUGAR YOU ADDED.

SOMETIMES I EAT TWO OR THREE BOWLS OF THIS.

I CAN HEAR YOUR HEART RACING FROM HERE.

THEY MAKE THIS CEREAL WITH MARSHMALLOW BITS, TOO, BUT MOM WON'T BUY IT FOR ME.

HEY, CALVIN! GUESS WHAT TIME IT IS!

WHY? WHAT TIME IS IT?

IT'S A VERY *SPECIAL* TIME!

OH BOY, OH BOY! WHAT TIME IS IT?

DO YOU *REALLY* WANT TO KNOW?

YES, YES! TELL ME! TELL ME! QUICK! PLEASE! YES!

IT'S YOUR BATH TIME! OH BOY!!

YOU KNOW HOW OLD PEOPLE ALWAYS WRITE TO DEAR ABBY, COMPLAINING THAT THEIR KIDS NEVER WRITE, CALL OR VISIT? THOSE LETTERS REALLY CRACK ME UP.

I HATE BEING A KID.

SOMEBODY'S ALWAYS TELLING YOU WHAT TO DO OR WHAT *NOT* TO DO. "DO THIS!" "STOP THAT!" DAY AFTER DAY.

YOU'RE LUCKY YOU'RE A TIGER.

WELL, WE TRY TO STAY HUMBLE, BUT LORD KNOWS IT'S HARD.

I WONDER IF I CAN GROW FANGS WHEN MY BABY TEETH FALL OUT.

I WISH *I* WAS A TIGER.

A COMMON LAMENT.

I'VE GOT AN IDEA! YOU CAN *TEACH* ME TO BE A TIGER! I'VE GOT SOME RED SLEEPERS I CAN WEAR! HANG ON!

SEE? WE CAN MAKE A TAIL BY STUFFING A KNEE SOCK AND PINNING IT ON MY REAR! THEN YOU CAN DRAW STRIPES ON MY FACE!

HMM... WHAT ABOUT FUR AND WHISKERS?

I HAVEN'T SHAVED FOR SIX YEARS. I SEEM TO BE CURSED WITH A THIN BEARD.

CALVIN and HOBBES

THE LATE CRETACEOUS PERIOD... WHEN DINOSAURS RULED THE EARTH!

by WATTERSON

..AND CALVIN RULED THE DINOSAURS!

THE TERRIBLE TYRANNOSAURUS SINKS ITS TEETH INTO A TRICERATOPS!

TRIUMPHANT AGAIN, THE UNDISPUTED KING OF DINOSAURS LETS OUT A MIGHTY ROAR!

WITH SAVAGE FEROCITY, THE MONSTER BEGINS ITS FEAST! LIMB-SEVERING, BONE-CRUNCHING AND TENDON-SNAPPING, HE...

CALVIN! THAT'S DISGUSTING!

FOR HEAVEN'S SAKE, SLOW DOWN AND CHEW QUIETLY!

THE TERRIBLE TYRANNOSAURUS RESUMES EATING, MORTIFIED THAT SOMEONE MIGHT SEE HIM.

145

LIGHTNING FLASHES! THUNDER RUMBLES ACROSS THE SKY!

HORRIBLY, CALVIN HAS BEEN SEWN TOGETHER FROM CORPSES! A POWER SURGE FORCES BLOOD TO HIS BRAIN!

HE'S... HE'S *ALIVE!*

WELL, LOOK WHO'S UP AND ABOUT.

HELLO, SLEEPYHEAD.

.OGGG...

CALVIN WAKES UP STARING INTO THE EYES OF A BIG FROG.

SEEING CALVIN AWAKE, THE FROG SCRAMBLES DOWN AND FORCES OPEN CALVIN'S MOUTH!

CALVIN TRIES TO FIGHT, BUT THE SLIPPERY AMPHIBIAN INSTANTLY SLIDES IN AND IS SWALLOWED! HOW DISGUSTING!

I DON'T FEEL GOOD.

YOU SOUND AWFUL. YOU'VE GOT A FROG IN YOUR THROAT.

CALVIN THE ELEPHANT WANDERS THE AFRICAN PLAIN.

AT FIVE TONS, HE IS THE LARGEST LAND MAMMAL!

HIS DEAFENING CALL SHATTERS THE EARLY-MORNING TRANQUILITY!

AHH! LUNCH, MY FAVORITE MEAL! AND TODAY'S LUNCH IS *EXTRA* SPECIAL!

EVER SINCE THE WEATHER GOT WARM I'VE BEEN SWATTING FLIES AND SAVING THEM IN A JAR.

FINALLY I GOT ENOUGH BUGS TO MASH THEM INTO A GOOEY PASTE WITH A SPOON.

I CALL IT "BUG BUTTER." CARE FOR A TASTE?

TELL ME, CALVIN, DO YOU HAVE ANY FRIENDS AT *ALL*?

OK, YOU'VE ALL READ THE CHAPTER, SO WHO CAN TELL ME WHAT'S IMPORTANT ABOUT THE BATTLE OF LEXINGTON?

ANYONE?

CALVIN, HOW ABOUT YOU?

HARD TO SAY, MA'AM. I THINK MY CEREBELLUM JUST FUSED.

HEY, MOM, CAN WE GO OUT FOR HAMBURGERS TONIGHT?

NOT TONIGHT, DEAR.

AW, MOM! WHY NOT?

BECAUSE I'M ALREADY FIXING SOMETHING FOR DINNER.

YEAH... I KNOW.

Calvin and Hobbes

by WATERSON

YAWWNN

DESPITE THAT AMAZING DISPLAY OF CUNNING, REFLEX AND PHYSICAL PROWESS, YOUR TAIL STILL HAS A DEATH GRIP ON YOUR BUTT.

COULD YOU STOP THE ROOM, PLEASE? I'D LIKE TO GET OFF.

WATERSON

BAD NEWS ON YOUR POLLS, DAD. YOU DROPPED ANOTHER FIVE POINTS.

IT SEEMS THAT ALTHOUGH YOUR RECOGNITION FACTOR IS HIGH, THE SCANDALS OF YOUR ADMINISTRATION CONTINUE TO HAUNT YOU.

SCANDALS? WHAT SCANDALS?!

BEDTIMEGATE AND HOMEWORKGATE COME READILY TO MIND.

INSTANCES OF TRUE LEADERSHIP. HISTORY WILL VINDICATE ME.

I WONDER WHAT MY NEW DAD WILL LOOK LIKE.

YOU'LL BE GLAD TO KNOW I'VE ANALYZED YOUR POOR SHOWING IN THE POLLS.

I'LL BET.

SEE, YOUR RECORD IN OFFICE IS MISERABLE AND THE CHARACTER ISSUE IS KILLING YOU. YOUR BASIC APPROVAL RATING AMONG SIX-YEAR-OLDS HARDLY REGISTERS.

IF ANYONE EVER NEEDED A SLICK AD CAMPAIGN, IT'S YOU.

LET ME GUESS WHAT YOU HAVE IN MIND.

"THE *NEW* DAD" I CALL IT.

I THINK THE IMAGE WE NEED TO CREATE FOR YOU IS, "REPENTANT, BUT LEARNING."

YOU KNOW, SHOW SOME HUMILITY, AND PRESENT YOURSELF AS A REGULAR GUY TRYING TO LEARN THE ROPES OF A DIFFICULT JOB.

DIFFICULT DOESN'T BEGIN TO DESCRIBE IT.

I WORKED UP SOME SLOGANS. SEE WHAT YOU THINK.

"DAD—GRADUALLY, HE CATCHES ON."
"VOTE DAD! *THIS* TIME, HE'LL DO BETTER."
"TO FORGIVE IS DIVINE—VOTE DAD IN '88."

I GET THE IDEA, CALVIN.

calvin and hobbes
by WATTERSON

YES, YOU CAN CERTAINLY SEE FAR FROM UP HERE.

I CALL THIS "LOOKOUT" HILL.

I CALL IT "LOOKOUT" HILL BECAUSE THAT'S WHAT YOU YELL WHENEVER WE GO DOWN IT.

YOU KNOW, SOMETIMES IT SEEMS THINGS GO BY TOO QUICKLY.

WE'RE SO BUSY WATCHING OUT FOR WHAT'S JUST AHEAD OF US THAT WE DON'T TAKE THE TIME TO ENJOY WHERE WE ARE.

DAYS GO BY AND WE HARDLY NOTICE THEM. LIFE BECOMES A BLUR.

OFTEN IT TAKES SOME CALAMITY TO MAKE US LIVE IN THE PRESENT.

THEN SUDDENLY WE WAKE UP AND SEE ALL THE MISTAKES WE'VE MADE, BUT IT'S TOO LATE TO CHANGE ANYTHING.

IT'S LIKE... ..IT'S LIKE...

IT'S LIKE WHAT?

IT'S LIKE SOMETHING... I JUST CAN'T THINK OF IT.

HERE I AM, WAITING FOR THE BUS. ELEVEN MORE YEARS OF SCHOOL TO GO. THEN COLLEGE, THEN MAYBE GRADUATE SCHOOL, AND THEN I WORK UNTIL I DIE.

WHAT KIND OF WORLD *IS* THIS?! YOU ONLY GET FIVE YEARS TO BE A KID??

WHAT ABOUT EXPLORING AND DISCOVERING AND PLAYING? THOSE THINGS ARE IMPORTANT, TOO!

WELL, YOU STILL HAVE AFTERNOONS AND WEEKENDS.

THAT'S WHEN I WATCH TV.

LOOK, HOBBES, I GOT A MODEL AIRPLANE. WANT TO HELP ME BUILD IT?

SURE.

WOW, A PHANTOM JET! I CAN'T WAIT UNTIL IT'S DONE!

LOOK AT ALL THE LITTLE PIECES.

HERE, YOU PUT THOSE PIECES TOGETHER, AND I'LL DO THESE. THEN WE'LL STICK YOURS ON MINE, OK?

SHOULDN'T WE READ THE INSTRUCTIONS?

DO I *LOOK* LIKE A SISSY?

HEY, THESE INSTRUCTIONS ARE IN THREE DIFFERENT LANGUAGES.

UH OH, I GOT GLUE ON MY HANDS.

IT STARTS IN ENGLISH, BUT THEN IT GOES INTO FRENCH AND SPANISH.

THIS STUFF IS WORSE THAN MOZZARELLA CHEESE.

IT'S HARD TO BELIEVE THIS MODEL IS FOR AGES SIX AND UP.

YECCHH. WHAT A MESS.

YOU HAVE TO BE TRI-LINGUAL JUST TO READ THE DIRECTIONS.

I HOPE MOM LIKES THIS NEWSPAPER HERE ON THE FLOOR, BECAUSE IT'S SURE NOT GOING ANYWHERE.

NUTS! THIS WHEEL STRUT SNAPPED. WHY DO THEY MAKE 'EM SO DARN SMALL?

I GUESS THAT WAS AN OPTIONAL PIECE.

MY WHEEL WON'T FIT IN THE WHEEL WELL.

HERE, LET ME TRY. SOMETIMES YOU JUST HAVE TO...

SNAP

DARN IT!

THIS PLANE IS IN FOR SOME ROUGH LANDINGS.

LOOK AT THIS STUPID MODEL. IT LOOKS AWFUL!

OUR PLANE DOESN'T LOOK ANYTHING LIKE THE PICTURE ON THE BOX.

MAYBE WE CAN FIX IT WHEN WE PAINT IT.

I CAN'T PAINT IT LIKE THIS. LOOK HOW GOOD THEY DID THIS!

Phantom

HOW'D THEY PAINT EYEBROWS ON A PILOT THAT'S LESS THAN AN INCH TALL ??

I THINK THAT'S A REAL JET SUPERIMPOSED ON A PLASTIC STAND.

I HATE THIS MODEL. NOTHING FIT RIGHT, THE INSTRUCTIONS WERE INCOMPREHENSIBLE, THE DECALS RIPPED, THE PAINT SLOPPED, AND THE GLUE GOT EVERYWHERE.

WHAT A DISASTER. SIX BUCKS COMPLETELY DOWN THE DRAIN.

I CAN'T THINK OF AN AFTERNOON I'VE ENJOYED LESS. WHAT A WASTE. WHAT A DUMB HOBBY.

..OF COURSE, WITH THIS FOR PRACTICE, I'LL BET WE COULD DO GREAT ON *ANOTHER* MODEL!

LET'S GET ONE OF THOSE CLIPPER SHIPS WITH ALL THE RIGGINGS.

I'M NOT GOING TO BED! I DON'T HAVE TO DO WHAT YOU SAY! I CAN DO ANYTHING I WANT!

..UH... HEH HEH

ENJOY THIS WHILE YOU CAN! I'LL BE A HULKING, SURLY TEEN-AGER BEFORE YOU KNOW IT!!

DID YOU EVER WONDER IF THE PERSON IN THE PUDDLE IS REAL, AND YOU'RE JUST A REFLECTION OF *HIM*?

IF THAT WAS TRUE, YOU'D DISAPPEAR AS SOON AS THE PERSON IN THE PUDDLE MOVED AWAY FROM THE PUDDLE, RIGHT?

GEE, I GUESS SO. I HADN'T THOUGHT OF THAT.

BANG!

BANG! BANG!

HA! THAT'S SIX SHOTS! YOU'RE OUT OF BULLETS! I'VE GOT YOU NOW, YOU RUSTLER!

ZAP!

"ZAP"?

MY CATTLE PROD.

HEY, SUSIE, GUESS WHAT I HAVE IN MY HANDS!

IS IT DISGUSTING?

UM... ..WELL...

IS IT SOME CREEPY, GOOEY THING THAT NO ONE IN HIS RIGHT MIND WOULD EVER, EVER WANT TO LOOK AT?

UH... I. I SUPPOSE THAT DEPENDS ON YOUR POINT OF VIEW...

FORGET IT. I'M NOT GUESSING.

YOU MIGHT AS WELL. YOU'RE NINE-TENTHS THERE.

MOM, WAS I EVER A GRUB?

A WHAT?

YOU KNOW, A LARVA. DID I REALLY PUPATE AT AGE TWO?

DON'T BE DISGUSTING! OF COURSE NOT! WHERE DID YOU EVER GET THAT AWFUL IDEA?!

YOU SHOULD GET YOUR STORIES STRAIGHT WITH MOM, MR. BRITANNICA!

HOW CAN YOU STAND THESE CARTOONS?

THEY'RE JUST HALF-HOUR COMMERCIALS FOR TOYS. AND WHEN THEY'RE NOT BORING, THEY'RE PREACHY.

AND THESE CHARACTERS DON'T EVEN *MOVE*. THEY JUST STAND AROUND BLINKING! WHAT KIND OF CARTOON IS *THAT*?

MEET MY DAD, THE GENE SISKEL OF SATURDAY MORNING TV.

CaLViN and HobbES

by WATTERSON

C'MON, HOBBES. LET ME UP INTO THE TREE FORT.

SAY THE PASSWORD.

NO! YOU KNOW IT'S ME! LET ME UP!

YOU MAY BE SOME OTHER KID IN DISGUISE.

IT'S *ME*, CALVIN! LET ME UP, YOU HAIRBALL BARFER!

AN INSULT! WELL, YOU CAN JUST STAY DOWN THERE *FOREVER*, MR. STINKER.

OH, NO! HERE COMES SUSIE! LET ME UP QUICK, SO WE CAN THROW THINGS AT HER! HURRY! LET DOWN THE ROPE!

LA DE DA DUM DOO ♪ ♫

SHE'S COMING! QUICK! LET DOWN THE ROPE! I'M SORRY I INSULTED YOU! OK? SEE, I SAID I WAS SORRY! CAN'T YOU LET DOWN THE ROPE?!

YOU HAVE TO SAY THE PASSWORD.

..*Verse Seven:* TIGERS ARE PERFECT, THE *E*-PIT-O-ME OF GOOD LOOKS AND GRACE AND QUIET..UH..UM..DIGNITY.

I WAS GOING TO ASK YOU TO COME OVER AND PLAY HOUSE, BUT I THINK YOU'D BE A WEIRD EXAMPLE FOR OUR CHILDREN.

ONE OF THESE DAYS I'M GOING TO MAKE YOU INTO A RUG! YOU HEAR ME?? A RUG!

CAN I USE THE GARDEN SHOVEL?

WHAT DO YOU WANT IT FOR?

HOBBES AND I ARE GOING ON AN ARCHAEOLOGICAL EXPEDITION.

IF YOU'RE LOOKING FOR FOSSILIZED REMAINS, YOU SHOULD DIG THROUGH YOUR ROOM.

HA HA. SOMEDAY I'LL NAME AN AUSTRALOPITHECUS WOMAN AFTER YOU.

I'VE BEEN READING UP ON PALEONTOLOGY. IT'S AMAZING STUFF.

SCIENTISTS CAN TELL HOW OLD SOMETHING IS JUST BY ANALYZING THE LAYERS OF DIRT IT'S IN.

HEY!

WHY, YOU MUST BE SIX YEARS OLD.

OH, YOU'RE A SCREAM.

ARCHAEOLOGISTS DIG SLOWLY AND CAREFULLY, USING SMALL, DELICATE TOOLS.

EACH ROCK HAS TO BE PAINSTAKINGLY BRUSHED AND SCRAPED SO NOTHING IS BROKEN OR MISSED.

DIG DIG SCRAPE SCRAPE BRUSH BRUSH

ARCHAEOLOGISTS HAVE THE MOST MIND-NUMBING JOB ON THE PLANET.

I DON'T THINK YOUR DAD WILL WANT TO SHAVE WITH THIS TOMORROW.

GOSH, LOOK AT ALL THE DINOSAUR BONES WE DISCOVERED.

LET'S GLUE THEM TOGETHER SO WE CAN SEE HOW THEY FIT. THEN YOU CAN DRAW A RECONSTRUCTION OF THE ACTUAL DINOSAUR.

AFTER THAT, WE'LL WRITE UP OUR FINDINGS, AND GET THEM PUBLISHED IN A SCIENTIFIC JOURNAL.

THEN WE'LL WIN THE NOBEL PRIZE, GET RICH, AND GO ON TALK SHOWS.

WHAT ABOUT BABES? WHEN DO WE GET THOSE?

WELL, HERE'S THE COMPLETE SKELETON AS NEAR AS *I* CAN FIGURE OUT.

TRY TO DRAW THE DINOSAUR AS IT REALLY LOOKED WITH MUSCLES AND SKIN.

RIGHT.

WHAT'S IT DOING? WHISTLING?

YOU TELL ME. MAYBE IT'S PUCKERING UP.

SEE THE DINOSAUR SKELETON WE DISCOVERED AND ASSEMBLED?

I'M GOING TO CALL THE NATURAL HISTORY MUSEUM AND TELL THEM THEY CAN HAVE IT FOR TEN BILLION DOLLARS.

THOSE ARE ...UM... PECULIAR BONES.

DO YOU THINK I SHOULD ASK FOR MORE MONEY?

THAT'S NOT *QUITE* WHAT I MEANT.

Calvin and Hobbes

by WATTERSON

THE CALL GOES OUT! WE'RE ON THE MOVE!

UP THROUGH THE WINDING MAZE! FASTER! FASTER!

CALVIN SCRAMBLES UP THE GRAINY TUNNEL!

OUT HE POPS INTO THE BLINDING SUN! CALVIN THE ANT RUSHES DOWN THE HILL TO THE BRICK WALK!

OTHER ANTS RUSH AROUND HIM IN THEIR MAD HURRY! CALVIN TRIES TO KEEP UP!

AT LAST HE REACHES THE MONSTROUS DEAD CATERPILLAR! WITHOUT PAUSING, HE HOISTS IT UP!

THE QUEEN DEMANDS HIS TIRELESS TOIL! CALVIN IS BACK OFF TO THE ANT-HILL AS FAST AS HE CAN GO!

WORK, WORK, WORK! THAT'S ALL I'M GOOD FOR AROUND HERE!

I HARDLY THINK PICKING UP YOUR ROOM ONCE IN A WHILE QUALIFIES YOU AS A SLAVE.

WATTERSON

CALVIN and HOBBES
by WATTERSON

THIS IS CALVIN, YOUR CAPTAIN, SPEAKING...

...JUST TO REASSURE YOU THAT, YES, THERE IS SOMEONE UP FRONT.

CALVIN PILOTS THE JET AIRLINER ACROSS THE COUNTRY AT 35,000 FEET.

HE IS GIVEN CLEARANCE TO LAND. BUT WHAT'S THIS? A PLANE FROM A RIVAL AIRLINE IS MAKING FOR THE SAME RUNWAY TO SHAVE PRECIOUS MINUTES OFF ITS SCHEDULE!

IT'S A 600-MPH GAME OF CHICKEN! CALVIN PULLS BACK ON THE THROTTLE AND LURCHES AHEAD!

THE OTHER PILOT TRIES TO CUT CALVIN OFF WITH A SUDDEN DROP IN ALTITUDE!

CALVIN SWITCHES ON THE "FASTEN SEAT BELT" LIGHT IN THE CABIN, AND DOES A BARREL ROLL!

AT 5 Gs, CALVIN HOPES NOT TO BLACK OUT!

AS THEY CLOSE IN ON THE RUNWAY, THE OTHER PILOT HAS NO CHOICE BUT TO PULL UP AND CIRCLE AROUND AGAIN! CALVIN WINS!

HEY, MOM, IS IT TRUE I COULD GET A PILOT'S LICENSE AT AGE 14?

NO.

I HAD NO *IDEA* BINOCULARS WERE SO EXPENSIVE! WE'RE DOOMED! WE'RE DOOMED!

"WE"?

WHY IN THE WORLD DID DAD LET ME USE ANYTHING SO VALUABLE?! HE SHOULD'VE *KNOWN* I'D BREAK THEM! HE MUST'VE BEEN OUT OF HIS MIND! THIS IS ALL *HIS* FAULT!

WHAT AM I GONNA *DO*!?

I SUPPOSE YOU *COULD* JUST TELL HIM WHAT HAPPENED...

..AND MAKE MY GETAWAY WHEN THE CORONARY HITS? SAY, *THAT'S* AN IDEA!

MAYBE WE COULD *GLUE* DAD'S BINOCULARS BACK TOGETHER AND HE WOULDN'T EVEN NOTICE! YOU THINK?

IT DEPENDS. WAS THE CASING JUST CHIPPED A LITTLE, OR DID THE LENS ITSELF GET CRACKED?

WELL, MAYBE YOU'D BETTER LOOK AT IT.

DON'T SNEEZE.

MAYBE YOU SHOULD TELL YOUR *MOM* ABOUT THE BINOCULARS, AND SHE CAN HELP SOMEHOW.

TELL MOM?!? ARE YOU CRAZY?? NO WAY!

WHY NOT? YOU'VE GOT TO TELL *SOMEONE*. MAYBE SHE CAN THINK OF SOMETHING.

AT TIMES LIKE THESE, ALL MOM CAN THINK OF IS HOW LONG SHE WAS IN LABOR WITH ME.

LOOK AT DAD, CALMLY EATING HIS DINNER AS IF NOTHING WAS WRONG.

I KNOW HIM. HIS "DAD RADAR" IS BEEPING LIKE CRAZY. HE KNOWS I BROKE *SOMETHING*, HE JUST DOESN'T KNOW *WHAT*. HE CAN'T NAIL ME UNTIL HE KNOWS FOR SURE. HE'LL JUST WAIT. I KNOW HIM.

HE'S GOING TO JUST SIT THERE EATING AND LET ME STEW IN MY OWN GUILT. HE FIGURES SOONER OR LATER I'LL CRACK.

CALVIN?

AAUGH! I DID IT! I DID IT! I'M SORRY! I DIDN'T MEAN TO!!

..PASS THE UH.. ..THE UH...

YOU *BROKE* THE BINOCULARS?!

DIDN'T I TELL YOU TO BE EXTRA, EXTRA CAREFUL WITH THEM?? ISN'T THAT EXACTLY WHAT I SAID? WELL?!

THOSE BINOCULARS WERE BRAND NEW! HAVE YOU NO RESPECT FOR OTHER PEOPLE'S PROPERTY.?!?

I HAVE AN IDEA, DAD. LET'S PRETEND I ALREADY FEEL TERRIBLE ABOUT IT, AND THAT YOU DON'T NEED TO RUB IT IN ANY MORE.

I DIDN'T *MEAN* TO BREAK YOUR BINOCULARS, DAD. IT WAS AN ACCIDENT.

(SNIFF) I'M REALLY SORRY. I FELT LIKE I WAS GOING TO BARF ALL AFTERNOON.

WELL, I'M SORRY I YELLED AT YOU LIKE I DID. I SHOULDN'T HAVE BEEN SO ANGRY.

AFTER ALL, IT WAS JUST A PAIR OF BINOCULARS. IN THE BIG SCHEME OF THINGS, THAT'S REALLY NOT SO BAD.

(SNIFF) REALLY?

SURE. ...IN ANOTHER TEN YEARS, YOU'LL PROBABLY BE WRECKING MY *CAR*.

HOBBES, LOOK! DAD GOT ME MY OWN PAIR OF LITTLE BINOCULARS!

WOW, THESE ARE *YOURS*?

AREN'T THEY GREAT?

I'LL SAY.

DAD SAID AS LONG AS I WAS GOING TO BREAK BINOCULARS, I OUGHT TO AT LEAST BREAK MY OWN.

NOW WE CAN GO TO THE BEACH AND LOOK AT BABES!

MAYBE I SHOULD BREAK DAD'S POWER TOOLS AND SEE IF I COULD GET SOME OF *THOSE*.

WIND WIND WIND

RUMBLE RUMBLE

EITHER I'M GREATLY DECEIVED, OR SOMEONE OPENED A CAN OF TUNA IN THIS VICINITY!

YES... ALL OVER THIS VICINITY.

WHAT A CLEAR NIGHT! LOOK AT ALL THE STARS. MILLIONS OF THEM!

YES, WE'RE JUST TINY SPECS ON A PLANET PARTICLE, HURLING THROUGH THE INFINITE BLACKNESS.

LET'S GO IN AND TURN ON ALL THE LIGHTS.

CALVIN and HOBBES by WATTERSON

ZZZZZZZZZZZZZZZ

FILTH! CONTAMINATION! PESTILENCE! HA HA HA!

OF ALL LIVING CREATURES, FEW ARE MORE REPULSIVE THAN CALVIN THE BUG!

HE EXISTS ONLY TO SUCK BLOOD AND TRANSMIT PARASITIC DISEASE!

SEARCHING FOR SOMEONE TO INFECT, CALVIN FLIES LOW OVER THE PICNIC TABLE!

Ton

INGREDIENTS: SALT,

HIS SENSITIVE ANTENNAE PICK UP THE SCENT OF HUMAN FLESH!

TOUCHING DOWN, CALVIN INSERTS HIS NEEDLELIKE PROBOSCIS INTO A VEIN! PROTOZOANS IN HIS SALIVA QUICKLY INDUCE PLAGUE!

WILL YOU STOP THAT AWFUL SLURPING?! YOU'RE MAKING ME SICK!

FWOOOOSH

AS IF LIFE ISN'T SHORT ENOUGH.

YOU KNOW WHAT WE NEED, HOBBES? WE NEED AN ATTITUDE.

AN ATTITUDE?

YEAH. YOU CAN'T BE COOL IF YOU DON'T HAVE AN ATTITUDE.

REALLY?

SURE. THEY'RE ALL THE RAGE. NOW WHAT KIND OF ATTITUDE COULD *WE* HAVE?

WE COULD BE COURTEOUSLY DEFERENTIAL.

OH, GOOD. THAT'S *REAL* COOL.

I'VE DECIDED TO BE A FATALIST.

ALL EVENTS ARE PREORDAINED AND UNALTERABLE. WHATEVER WILL BE WILL BE. THAT WAY, IF ANYTHING BAD HAPPENS, IT'S NOT MY FAULT. IT'S FATE.

TRIP

WAUGH

TOO BAD YOU WERE FATED TO DO THAT.

THAT WASN'T FATE!

DO YOU THINK GROWN-UPS WILL HAVE THE WORLD FIXED UP BY THE TIME THEY HAND IT OVER TO US?

NOT THE WAY THEY'RE GOING.

THAT'S WHAT *I* THOUGHT.

I GUESS THAT MEANS IT'S UP TO *US* THEN.

SOMEHOW, I'M NOT REASSURED.

HA! WHEN *I'M* PRESIDENT, I'LL HAVE THINGS WHIPPED INTO SHAPE IN NO TIME.

HEY, LOOK! MOM AND DAD ARE THROWING DUFFEL BAGS IN THE CAR. THEY'RE GOING ON VACATION!

AT LAST! FINALLY WE GET THE HOUSE TO OURSELVES! WE CAN STAY UP LATE AND WATCH TV! WE CAN EAT COOKIES FOR DINNER! WE...

WHAT ARE YOU DOING UP HERE STILL? C'MON, LET'S GO.

ME? GO? GO WHERE?

ON VACATION! WHAT HAVE WE BEEN PLANNING ALL MONTH?

WITH YOU AND MOM?? WHAT KIND OF VACATION IS *THAT*?!

SO WHERE ARE WE GOING? I SURE HOPE WE'RE NOT CAMPING AGAIN THIS YEAR.

WELL, WE ARE.

OH, NO! WHY DO WE HAVE TO GO CAMPING?! I *HATE* CAMPING!

SWATTING MOSQUITOES WHILE LYING FROZEN AND CRAMPED ON BUMPY ROCKS, WITH NO TV AND ONLY CANNED FOOD TO EAT, IS *NOT* MY IDEA OF A GOOD TIME!

THAT'S WHY WE BROUGHT BUG SPRAY.

LOOK, JUST LET ME OUT HERE, OK? I'LL HITCH HOME AND SEE YOU WHEN YOU GET BACK, ALL RIGHT?

REMEMBER LAST YEAR, WHEN IT RAINED ALL WEEK? IT POURED SO HARD WE COULDN'T EVEN MAKE A FIRE.

WITHOUT QUESTION, THAT WAS ONE OF THE WORST EXPERIENCES OF MY LIFE.

YES, BUT IT BUILT CHARACTER.

OH SURE.

WHY CAN'T I EVER BUILD CHARACTER AT A MIAMI CONDO OR A CASINO SOMEWHERE?

WELL, HERE WE ARE! HOME AWAY FROM HOME!

OK, CALVIN, YOU GET OUT WITH YOUR MOM, AND I'LL HAND OUR GEAR TO YOU.

NOW DON'T DROP THIS. IT'S VERY...

OOPS.

PLOONK

DON'T WORRY, DAD. IT'S ONLY ABOUT TEN FEET DEEP. I CAN SEE THE CAMERA AND EVERYTHING.

I AM GOING TO FEED YOU TO THE SEA GULLS, KID.

DEAR, YOU CAME HERE TO *RELAX*.

GOSH, THIS WATER'S COLD! HERE, THAT'S ALL I COULD FIND DOWN THERE. GO GET ME A TOWEL, CALVIN.

IT NEVER FAILS. THE ONE BAG THE KID DUMPS IN THE DRINK HAS ALL THE FRAGILE AND PERISHABLE ITEMS IN IT.

WELL, THE WEEK CAN ONLY IMPROVE FROM HERE.

ONE WOULD LIKE TO *THINK* SO.

HEY, DAD, DID YOU MEAN TO STACK THE TACKLE BOX AND ALL THIS ON YOUR GLASSES?

BOY, DON'T GO NEAR DAD. WHAT A GROUCH!

I DON'T SEE WHY HE CAN'T BE CIVIL JUST BECAUSE I ACCIDENTALLY DROPPED A DUFFEL BAG OVERBOARD AND HE BROKE HIS GLASSES.

ARE YOU GOING TO TELL HIM HE LEFT THE CAR LIGHTS ON BACK WHERE WE GOT THE CANOE?

I THINK *YOU* SHOULD TELL HIM.

HEY, MOM, DAD AND I ARE GOING FISHING. DON'T YOU WANT TO COME ALONG?

UGGH, NO. THE LAST THING I WANT TO SEE AT THIS UNGODLY HOUR IS A BUNCH OF SLIMY FISH GASPING AND FLOPPING IN THE SLOP AT THE BOTTOM OF A BOAT.

ALL *I'D* LIKE TO SEE IS A DECENT NEWSPAPER, A FRESH MUFFIN AND A POT OF REAL COFFEE.

WHY'D WE EVER COME *HERE* THEN?

GO ASK CONAN THE BARBARIAN.

C'MON, CALVIN. I'LL TEACH YOU TO PUT A WORM ON A HOOK.

AHHH, WHAT A DAY!

UP AT DAWN! FRESH AIR! TRANQUILITY! NO DEMANDS, NO PHONES, NO PRESSURE!

THE WHOLE DAY IS ONE'S OWN! ISN'T THIS GREAT? ISN'T THIS THE LIFE?

SPACEMAN SPIFF, A PRISONER ON THE ZOG SLAVE GALLEY, PLANS HIS DARING OVERBOARD ESCAPE!

AHH, WHAT A DAY!

GOSH, I COULD LOOK AT THE STARS ALL NIGHT.

WITHOUT THE STREETLIGHTS OR POLLUTION HERE, IT SEEMS LIKE YOU CAN SEE FOREVER INTO SPACE.

SNAP CRUNCH

OF COURSE, IF YOU'VE SEEN ONE STAR, YOU'VE SEEN THEM ALL.

TRUE, TRUE. SHALL WE MOSEY ON BACK TO THE TENT?

LOOK, MOM, THE WATER IS UP TO MY KNEES!

SEE? SEE? LOOK, MOM! THE WATER'S UP TO MY KNEES! SEE? LOOK WHERE THE WATER IS!

NOW LOOK! THE WATER IS *HIGHER* THAN MY KNEES! SEE? LOOK, MOM! SEE?

I'M ENTHRALLED, CALVIN.

YOU'RE NOT EVEN *LOOKING!*

WHATCHA DOIN', DAD? PAINTING A PICTURE?

YEP.

WHAT'S THAT THING? A BRONTOSAURUS WITH RABIES?

IT'S THAT ISLAND OVER THERE.

OH.

HOW FAR CAN YOU SEE WITHOUT YOUR GLASSES? CAN YOU SEE *ME*?

WHEN I LOOK UP, I'D BETTER NOT BE ABLE TO.

HI, MOM!

MM.

DAD'S PAINTING A PICTURE, BUT IT'S NOT COMING OUT SO HOT, AND HE'S IN A REALLY STINKY MOOD. IT'S LIKE, I ASKED HIM ONE LITTLE QUESTION AND HE NEARLY BIT MY HEAD OFF! I MEAN, IT'S NOT AS IF *I* RUINED HIS LOUSY PICTURE, RIGHT? WHY SHOULD...

CALVIN, CAN'T YOU SEE I'M TRYING TO READ?

EVER NOTICE HOW TENSE GROWN-UPS GET WHEN THEY'RE RECREATING?

THERE'S NOTHING TO *DO* HERE.

THAT'S SORT OF THE POINT, DON'T YOU THINK? IT'S GOOD TO STOP RUNNING AROUND.

SOMETIMES ONE SHOULD JUST LOOK AT THINGS AND THINK ABOUT THINGS, WITHOUT *DOING* THINGS.

YOU'RE CERTAINLY THE EXPERT ON *THAT*.

WHAT I LIKE IS WHEN YOU'RE LOOKING AND THINKING AND LOOKING AND THINKING....AND SUDDENLY YOU WAKE UP.

MOM, CAN HOBBES COME IN SWIMMING WITH ME?

I DON'T THINK HE'D BETTER, CALVIN.

WHY NOT?

UM... TIGERS DON'T SWIM VERY WELL.

THEY DON'T?

FRANKLY, I'M NOT SURE YOUR MOM KNOWS SO MUCH ABOUT TIGERS.

LOOK, WE JUST WANT TO AVOID AN ARGUMENT, RIGHT?

OK, CALVIN, START PACKING UP. WE'RE GOING HOME.

FINALLY!

NOW, NOW. THESE LITTLE OUTINGS ARE VALUABLE EXPERIENCES.

YEAH? HOW?

THEY GIVE US A CHANCE TO BE TOGETHER AS A FAMILY AND LEARN ABOUT OURSELVES.

LIKE HOW WE CAN'T STAND BEING IN SUCH CLOSE PROXIMITY WITH ONE ANOTHER THIS LONG?

EXACTLY.

THIS PROBABLY JUST GOES TO SHOW SOMETHING, BUT I SURE DON'T KNOW WHAT.

THERE'S QUITE A BREEZE UP HERE. I'M REALLY MOVING. THERE'S THE RIVER AND THE TOWN TRIANGLE.

HEY, DOWN THERE! MY NAME IS CALVIN! TELL MY TIGER, HOBBES, I'M BLOWING AWAY ON A BALLOON!

CAN ANYONE HEAR ME? TELL HOBBES HE CAN'T READ MY COMIC BOOKS JUST 'CAUSE I'M NOT AROUND, OK?

...OH, YEAH, TELL MY PARENTS WHAT HAPPENED, TOO, ALL RIGHT? HELLO? HELLO?

UH OH, I'M HEADING INTO A FLOCK OF DUCKS!

EXCUSE ME! COMING THROUGH!

PARDON ME! GANGWAY! BEEP BEEP!

...BOY, IF LOOKS COULD KILL.

THIS HAS GOT TO BE A DREAM.

WHENEVER YOU FALL FROM TWO MILES UP IN THE SKY, YOU LOOK DOWN, GASP, AND SUDDENLY WAKE UP.

GASP!

GASP
GASP
GASP
GASP
GASP

I WONDER IF MY LIFE WILL FLASH BEFORE MY EYES.

THAT'S THE PROBLEM WITH BEING SIX YEARS OLD...

...MY LIFE WON'T TAKE VERY LONG TO WATCH.

MAYBE I CAN GET A FEW SLOW-MOTION REPLAYS OF THE TIME I SMACKED SUSIE UPSIDE THE HEAD WITH A SLUSHBALL.

SAY, I WONDER IF I HAVE ANY GUM IN MY POCKET. I COULD BLOW A BIG BUBBLE, AND...

NOPE, NO GUM. LET'S TRY *THIS* POCKET.

MY TRANSMOGRIFIER GUN!!

BOY, THESE THINGS COME IN HANDY ALL THE TIME.

I FORGOT ALL ABOUT MY TRANSMOGRIFIER GUN! NOW I HAVE NOTHING TO WORRY ABOUT!

I'LL JUST POINT IT AT MYSELF AND TRANSMOGRIFY! I'M SAFE!

ZAP

WHERE HAVE YOU BEEN?? I'VE BEEN CALLING AND CALLING. YOUR DINNER'S COLD, I'M SURE.

I DRIFTED AWAY ON MY BALLOON AND IT POPPED, BUT FORTUNATELY I HAD MY TRANSMOGRIFIER, SO AFTER I MISTAKENLY TURNED MYSELF INTO A SAFE, I TRANSMOGRIFIED INTO A LIGHT PARTICLE AND ZIPPED BACK HOME INSTANTANEOUSLY!

...OF COURSE, IF I'D KNOWN WE WERE HAVING **THIS**, I WOULDN'T HAVE HURRIED.

SOMETIME YOU SHOULD TRY TRANSMOGRIFYING YOURSELF INTO SOMEONE WHO OCCASIONALLY MAKES AN OUNCE OF SENSE.

CALVIN, I'D LIKE YOU TO PICK UP ALL THE STICKS AND FALLEN BRANCHES IN THE YARD, SO I CAN MOW IT.

WILL YOU PAY ME?

WELL... OK, I'LL PAY YOU A DOLLAR.

A DOLLAR? I WON'T DO IT FOR LESS THAN TWENTY-FIVE!!

IN A MINUTE YOU'LL DO IT FOR NOTHING, JUST BECAUSE I TOLD YOU TO.

...I'LL TAKE THE DOLLAR.

SMART KID.

CALVIN and HOBBES
by WATTERSON

SPACEMAN SPIFF EXPLORES THE OUTERMOST REACHES OF THE UNIVERSE.

BY POPULAR REQUEST.

INTREPID EXPLORER SPACEMAN SPIFF LANDS ON AN UNCHARTED PLANET. WHAT STRANGE WONDERS WILL HE DISCOVER HERE?

SPIFF SETS OUT IN SEARCH OF SENTIENT LIFE!

WHAT A STRANGE PLANET THIS IS! ITS SURFACE IS SURPRISINGLY SOFT AND POROUS!

AND HERE CURIOUS GEYSERS BLAST HOT AIR!

SUDDENLY IT DAWNS ON HIM! SPIFF IS NOT ON THE PLANET'S SURFACE AT ALL! HE'S WALKING ON A RECLINING ALIEN!!

OUR HERO SETS HIS DEATH RAY BLASTER.

ZZ.. MMF HM?

LET'S GO, CALVIN! WE'RE ALL READY!

BOY, I HAVEN'T BEEN TO THE ZOO IN AGES.

AND CALVIN'S NEVER BEEN. THIS WILL BE FUN.

I'VE BEEN TELLING HIM ABOUT IT ALL WEEK. HE'S SO EXCITED.

C'MON, CALVIN!

SO *WHERE* DO WE HAVE TO GO NOW?

BEATS *ME*. MOM AND DAD ARE ALWAYS DRAGGING US *SOME* DUMB PLACE.

HOW COME THE ALLIGATORS ARE IN THIS BIG PIT?

SO THEY DON'T GET OUT AND EAT PEOPLE.

DOES THE ZOO EVER THROW ANYONE IN?

DON'T BE SILLY. OF COURSE NOT.

HOW SOON UNTIL WE GO HOME?

LOOK! MONKEYS!

SEE HOW THEY USE THEIR TAILS AND FEET TO CLIMB?

ZOOS LET PEOPLE SEE HOW WILD ANIMALS REALLY BEHAVE.

HEY, LOOK WHAT *THAT* MONKEY'S DOING! RIGHT IN PUBLIC, TOO! HA HA! THAT'S GROSS! HOW COME *I'M* NOT ALLOWED TO DO THAT?!

COME LOOK AT THE BIRDS OVER HERE, CALVIN.

196

HERE'S HOBBES, BUT WHERE'S CALVIN?

I DON'T SEE HIM.

WHERE COULD HE HAVE GONE? WE JUST TURNED OUR BACKS FOR A MINUTE.

AND WHY DIDN'T HE TAKE HOBBES?

YOU STAY HERE IN CASE HE COMES BACK, AND I'LL GO LOOK FOR HIM.

OK. (SIGH)

BEING A PARENT IS WANTING TO HUG AND STRANGLE YOUR KID AT THE SAME TIME.

SHEESH. CALVIN COULD BE ANYWHERE IN THIS ZOO.

I HOPE HE AT LEAST HAS THE SENSE TO STAY PUT, WHEREVER HE IS.

WHERE WOULD THE LITTLE ROTTER GO IF HE WAS LOST AND SEPARATED FROM HIS STUFFED TOY?

HIS NAME IS HOBBES, AND HE'S... HEY, I'M TALKING TO YOU!!

TIGERS
Panthera tigris

I KNOW! MAYBE CALVIN'S AT THE TIGER PIT, SINCE HE LIKES TIGERS SO MUCH.

HA HA, MAYBE CALVIN'S *IN* THE TIGER PIT, SINCE HE LIKES TIGERS SO MUCH.

YOU FOUND HIM! THANK GOODNESS! WHERE WAS HE?

LOOKING AT THE TIGERS.

I FOLLOWED ANOTHER LADY, THINKING IT WAS MOM, AND THEN WHEN I REALIZED I WAS LOST, I WENT TO ASK THE TIGERS IF THEY'D SEEN HOBBES.

NEXT TIME YOU SHOULD ASK A *PERSON* FOR HELP.

...OH... THAT NEVER OCCURRED TO ME.

ONLY NEXT TIME, THERE WON'T *BE* A NEXT TIME, BECAUSE WE'RE JUST GOING TO TIE YOU TO A STAKE IN THE YARD EVERY WEEKEND.

DEAR!

A FAT LOT OF HELP YOUR COMPATRIOTS WERE, I MIGHT ADD.

DO YOU KNOW WHAT DAY IT IS?

NOPE. WHY?

OH, NO REASON. I WAS JUST CURIOUS.

I SURE LIKE SUMMER VACATION.

SO YOU WANT SOME WATER, HUH? WELL, I'VE GOT A BIG CAN OF IT HERE.

IT'S UP TO *ME* TO DECIDE IF YOU GET WATER OR NOT! *I* CONTROL YOUR FATE! YOUR VERY *LIVES* ARE IN MY HANDS!

WITHOUT *ME* YOU'RE AS GOOD AS DEAD! WITHOUT *ME*, YOU DON'T...

SAFE!

OK, THAT WAS A SINGLE. I HAVE A GHOST RUNNER HERE NOW, SO I CAN BAT AGAIN.

AND MY GHOST RUNNERS WHO *WERE* ON FIRST AND SECOND BASE ARE NOW ON SECOND AND THIRD, RIGHT?

NOPE. THEY'RE BOTH OUT.

OUT?!

MY GHOST OUTFIELDER TAGGED YOUR GHOST GOING TO THIRD, AND THREW TO MY GHOST SECOND BASEMAN. IT WAS A BRILLIANT DOUBLE PLAY.

THAT NEVER HAPPENED!

YOU'VE GOT TWO OUTS.

WELL, MY GHOST ON FIRST JUST STOLE HOME, SO I'VE GOT ANOTHER RUN! HA HA, SMARTY!

YEAH, WELL, ALL MY OUTFIELD GHOSTS JUST RAN IN AND BEAT THE TOBACCO JUICE OUT OF HIM.

HA! THE GHOST UMPIRE JUST SUSPENDED ALL YOUR GHOSTS FOR ETERNITY. THEY'RE OUT OF THE GAME.

HMPH! IF MY GHOSTS DON'T PLAY, *I* DON'T PLAY.

YOU FORFEIT THE GAME THEN! YOU LOSE AUTOMATICALLY IF YOU QUIT!

THE GHOST CROWD SUPPORTS ME. THEY'RE "BOO"-ING YOU!

SOMETIMES I WISH I LIVED IN A NEIGHBORHOOD WITH MORE KIDS.

199

CALViN and HObbEs by WATTERSON

RUSTLE
RUSTLE

ZING!

WHAM!

WE TIGERS JUST *LIVE* FOR THAT!

NOT FOR LONG, YOU WON'T.

BOY, WHAT A BEAUTIFUL SUMMER MORNING, HUH, DAD? TOO BAD YOU CAN'T STAY HOME TO ENJOY IT.

WHEN YOU'RE OLD, YOU'LL BE SORRY YOU NEVER TOOK ADVANTAGE OF DAYS LIKE THESE, BUT OF COURSE, THAT'S FAR OFF, AND IN THE MEANTIME, THERE'S LOTS OF WORK TO BE DONE.

YEP, YOU'D BETTER GO TO WORK. HAVE A GOOD LONG DRIVE IN TRAFFIC. MAYBE YOU'LL GET HOME IN TIME TO WATCH THE SUN SET... IF YOU CAN STAY AWAKE. SO LONG!

GOLLY, I'D HATE TO HAVE A KID LIKE ME.

WHAT WOULD YOU DO IF I CREAMED YOU WITH THIS WATER BALLOON RIGHT NOW?

TAKE THE WORST THING YOU CAN IMAGINE, AND IMAGINE SOMETHING A HUNDRED TIMES WORSE THAN THAT.

YOU'D DO *THAT*?

NO, I'D DO SOMETHING EVEN WORSE.

HE PIQUED MY CURIOSITY.

BIP

WHEEEE.

203

WHAT ARE YOU DOING WITH ALL YOUR DAD'S TOOLS IN THE BATHROOM?

THIS FAUCET DRIPS, SO I'M GOING TO FIX IT.

YOU'RE GOING TO FIX IT?

THAT'S WHAT I SAID.

..AND YOU CAN KEEP YOUR COMMENTS TO YOURSELF, DR. DOOM.

I DIDN'T SAY ANYTHING.

FIXING A FAUCET IS EASY. ALL YOU DO IS TAKE IT APART, SEE WHAT'S LEAKING, PLUG IT UP, AND PUT IT BACK TOGETHER.

DOES YOUR MOM KNOW YOU'RE DOING THIS?

NOPE. IT'S GOING TO BE A SURPRISE.

AND WE ALL KNOW HOW SHE LOVES SURPRISES.

I CAN'T GET THIS HANDLE OFF. PASS ME THE HACK-SAW, WILL YOU?

AREN'T YOU SUPPOSED TO TURN THE WATER OFF BEFORE YOU TAKE APART A FAUCET?

THAT'S THE PROBLEM I'M TRYING TO FIX, YOU MORON! I CAN'T TURN THE WATER OFF BECAUSE THE FAUCET LEAKS!

SHEESH, WHERE WERE *YOU* WHEN THEY WERE PASSING OUT BRAINS?

OH NO! AUGHH! ACKK!

I'LL GET YOU SOME PAPER AND CARBONS FOR YOUR WRITTEN APOLOGY.

WHAT'S ALL THAT WATER I HEAR? I'M COMING IN!

OH MY GOSH! ACKPBT! WHAT'S GOING ON?!? SPLUTB! BPLPTH!

THERE! I GOT THE WATER OFF. **ALL RIGHT, CALVIN, WHERE ARE YOU?!**

H-HI, DAD.

IT'S THE END OF THE WORLD, CALVIN.

LOOK AT THIS BATHROOM! WHAT ON EARTH WERE YOU *DOING*?!

NOTHING, DAD! I WAS JUST IN HERE LOOKING FOR SOME DENTAL FLOSS, WHEN *PLOOIE!* THE FAUCET HANDLE BLOWS SKY HIGH ALL BY ITSELF! IT...IT... UH...

WHAT I MEAN IS, HOBBES WAS FOOLING AROUND WITH YOUR TOOLS. I TRIED TO STOP HIM, BUT HE WOULDN'T LISTEN, AND SURE ENOUGH, HE WENT AND... AND...

ONE MORE TRY.

ALIENS, DAD! BIG, EVIL, BUG-EYED MONSTERS FROM PLUTO! THEY DID IT, AND MADE ME SWEAR NOT TO TELL!

BOY, DAD SURE BLEW HIS STACK *THAT* TIME, DIDN'T HE? WHAT A SOREHEAD!

LISTENING TO *HIM*, YOU'D THINK NOBODY IN THE WORLD HAD EVER NEEDED TO CALL A PLUMBER BEFORE. DAD'S GOT A JOB. HE CAN AFFORD IT.

DAD MAKES SUCH A BIG DEAL OUT OF EVERYTHING.

WHEN HE DOES, I SURE WISH YOU'D STOP TRYING TO PIN YOUR CRIMES ON *ME*.

OH, NOW *YOU'RE* GOING TO START IN ON ME *TOO*, HUH?

calvin and Hobbes by WATTERSON

DINOSAURS EVERYWHERE FLEE FOR THEIR LIVES!

CALVIN IS COMING!

THE LATE CRETACEOUS: THE LAST EPOCH OF THE MIGHTY DINOSAURS!

KING OF THE THUNDER LIZARDS IS THE FEARSOME CALVIN, THE TYRANNOSAURUS!

SEVEN TONS OF MUSCLE AND TEETH. HE SEARCHES FOR PREY!

CALVIN, FOR GOODNESS' SAKE, STOP STOMPING AROUND! YOU'RE DRIVING ME CRAZY!

OW!! CHOMP.

HOW DID THE FEARSOME TYRANNOSAURUS BECOME EXTINCT? NOW WE KNOW!

EVERYTHING FLOATS RANDOMLY IN THE ROOM! THERE'S NO GRAVITY!

CALVIN PUSHES OFF THE CEILING AT A SHARP ANGLE, AIMING FOR THE HALLWAY!

HE GLIDES WITH UNCHECKED MOMENTUM, TURNING HIMSELF TO BE ABLE TO PUSH OFF THE NEXT STATIONARY SURFACE.

C'MON, YOU! OUTSIDE! YOU'RE REALLY BOUNCING OFF THE WALLS TODAY.

AW, MOM.

EXTRA PANTS...

THREE SHIRTS, TWO SWEATERS, TWO SWEATSHIRTS...

ANOTHER PAIR OF PANTS...

STILL TRYING TO LEARN TO RIDE THAT BICYCLE, EH?

I DON'T NEED ANY COMMENTS FROM YOU.

A SHADOW FALLS OVER THE LARGE CITY SKYSCRAPERS!

IT'S A GIGANTIC ANT! WITH ONE FOOTSTEP, IT PULVERIZES THE ENTIRE DOWNTOWN! MILLIONS DIE INSTANTLY!

THE ANT BRUSHES THE CITY OFF THE MAP! PEOPLE FLOOD THE STREETS IN PANIC, ONLY TO BE SMASHED IN THE HORRIBLE WRECKAGE!

WELL... MAYBE I WON'T...

213

TRIP

BAP

WHACK

BAP

I'M HUNGRY.

TOO BAD. BREAKFAST ISN'T UNTIL TOMORROW.

MY TUMMY'S GROWLING.

HUSH.

MOST PEOPLE DON'T SLEEP WELL NEXT TO A HUNGRY TIGER.

SOMETIMES I SURE WISH I HAD A DOG.

MORE TUNA AND LESS MAYONNAISE.

OH, NO! THERE'S A TYRANNOSAURUS IN THE GROCERY STORE!

THE DINOSAUR HEADS FOR THE MEAT DEPARTMENT AND DEVOURS THE BUTCHER!

SHOPPERS EVERYWHERE FLEE FOR THEIR LIVES! IT'S MAYHEM, DESTRUCTION AND CARNAGE IN THE AISLES!

OH, NO! CALVIN, CAN'T I TAKE YOU ANYWHERE?!

NOW THE TYRANNOSAURUS WANTS COOKIES!

PLANET CALVIN MOVES ACROSS THE SOLAR SYSTEM.

NOBODY NOTICES UNTIL HIS ORBIT TAKES HIM DIRECTLY BETWEEN THE SUN AND EARTH.

CALVIN CAUSES A TOTAL SOLAR ECLIPSE! EARTH IS SHROUDED IN DARKNESS. HOW LONG WILL CALVIN STAY THERE?!

COULD YOU MOVE, PLEASE? YOU'RE IN MY LIGHT.

HA HA HAAA!

ELECTION DAY IS COMING UP. HAVE YOU DECIDED ON A RUNNING MATE?

A RUNNING MATE?

SURE. YOU CAN'T BE ELECTED DAD WITHOUT A MOM, RIGHT?

ARE YOU GOING TO KEEP THE MOM I'VE HAD, OR GET A *NEW* RUNNING MATE?

GEE...

BEDTIME, CALVIN.

OF COURSE I'LL STICK WITH YOUR MOM.

AWW...

I THINK RITUALS ARE IMPORTANT.

MY FAVORITE RITUAL IS EATING THREE BOWLS OF "CHOCOLATE FROSTED SUGAR BOMBS" AND WATCHING TV CARTOONS ALL SATURDAY MORNING.

AFTER A FEW HOURS, I'M SO OVERSTIMULATED I CAN'T SIT STILL OR EVEN THINK STRAIGHT.

SORT OF A TRANSCENDENTAL EXPERIENCE, HUH?

YEAH. I ACHIEVE A LOWER CONSCIOUSNESS.

I PLEDGE ALLEGIANCE...

TO QUEEN FRAGG... AND HER MIGHTY STATE OF HYSTERIA...

IT'S GOING TO BE A LONG YEAR.

Hey, Calvin, you're on my swing. Get lost.

I'M NOT SCARED OF YOU, MOE.

Oh no?

NOPE. YOU'RE SO DUMB YOU PROBABLY NEVER THOUGHT ABOUT HOW A SPARROW'S SMALLER SIZE AND GREATER MANEUVERABILITY IS AN ADVANTAGE IN FIGHTING OFF BIG CROWS.

Yeah?

PUNCH

THOSE TV NATURE PROGRAMS WILL BE THE DEATH OF ME YET.

YES, CALVIN?

MAY I BE EXCUSED, PLEASE?

AGAIN?

I HAVE TO GO. BAD.

ALL RIGHT.

THANK YOU.

WHAT ARE *YOU* DOING HOME?!

I HAD TO GO.

CalviN and HobbEs
by WATTERSON

SCHOOL'S OUT! FREE AT LAST!

AND JUST SIX PRECIOUS HOURS BEFORE BED TO FORGET EVERYTHING I LEARNED TODAY.

I HATE COMING HOME FROM SCHOOL. I NEVER KNOW IF HOBBES IS WAITING TO POUNCE ON ME.

MAYBE I CAN STAND OFF TO THE SIDE HERE, AND PUSH THE DOOR OPEN WITH A STICK.

I'M HOME!

WHAT DO YOU DO, WAIT UNTIL YOU SEE THE WHITES OF MY EYES?!?

BOY, YOU SHOULD'VE *SEEN* THEM! THEY WERE AS BIG AS DINNER PLATES! HOO HOO HOO!

HAVE YOU BEEN READING THE PAPERS? GROWN-UPS REALLY HAVE THE WORLD FOULED UP.

ACID RAIN, TOXIC WASTES, HOLES IN THE OZONE, SEWAGE IN THE OCEANS, AND ON AND ON!

THE ONLY BRIGHT SIDE TO ALL THIS IS THAT EVENTUALLY THERE MAY NOT BE A PIECE OF THE PLANET WORTH FIGHTING OVER.

YOU'RE PACKING?

YEP. GET YOUR TOOTHBRUSH, HOBBES. WE'RE OUTTA HERE.

IT'S AN OUTRAGE HOW GROWN-UPS HAVE POLLUTED THE EARTH! I REFUSE TO INHERIT A SPOILED PLANET! I'M LEAVING!

REALLY? WHERE TO??

YOU KNOW, SOMETIMES YOU'RE A REAL LOAD TO HAVE AROUND.

I WAS JUST ASKING!

HOW ABOUT MARS? WE COULD GO THERE TO AVOID EARTH'S POLLUTION.

YEAH! IF WE GO NOW, WE CAN CLAIM IT AND KEEP EVERYONE ELSE OFF IT.

OK, IT'S SETTLED. MARS IT IS.

YOU FINISH PACKING. I'LL GO GET THE WAGON.

WE'RE GOING IN THE WAGON?

OF COURSE! WHAT DID YOU WANT TO DO? FLAP YOUR ARMS?

I GUESS I HADN'T THOUGHT ABOUT THAT PART.

OBVIOUSLY.

SO LONG, MOM. HOBBES AND I ARE GOING TO MARS TO LIVE. EARTH IS TOO POLLUTED.

HAVE A GOOD TIME.

SAY GOODBYE TO DAD FOR US. IF I CAN FIND AN INTERPLANETARY POST OFFICE, I'LL WRITE YOU ONCE IN A WHILE AND...

CALVIN, DON'T STAND THERE WITH THE DOOR OPEN. YOU'RE LETTING IN BUGS. EITHER STAY IN OR GO OUTSIDE.

SHE DIDN'T SEEM TOO CHOKED UP ABOUT US GOING, DID SHE?

WE SHOULD'VE LEFT A LONG TIME AGO.

BLAST OFF!

DO YOU REALLY THINK WE'LL GET ENOUGH LIFT TO BREAK EARTH'S GRAVITY?

OF COURSE! YOU THINK I DIDN'T PLAN THIS OUT?! I THOUGHT OF EVERYTHING.

DID YOU THINK OF WHAT YOU'LL EAT ON OUR TRIP?

PACKING WAS YOUR JOB! DIDN'T YOU PACK US ANY FOOD??

I PACKED FOOD FOR ME...

WE DID IT! WE CLEARED EARTH'S ORBIT!

MARS, HERE WE COME!

ARE YOU SURE THIS IS THE WAY?

WHAT? DIDN'T YOU BRING THE MAP?!

SPACE TRAVEL MAKES YOU REALIZE JUST HOW SMALL WE REALLY ARE.

WHEN YOU SEE EARTH AS A TINY BLUE SPECK IN THE INFINITE REACHES OF SPACE, YOU HAVE TO WONDER ABOUT THE MYSTERIES OF CREATION.

SURELY WE'RE ALL PART OF SOME GREAT DESIGN, NO MORE OR LESS IMPORTANT THAN ANY-THING ELSE IN THE UNIVERSE. SURELY EVERYTHING FITS TOGETHER AND HAS A PURPOSE, A REASON FOR BEING. DOESN'T IT MAKE YOU WONDER?

I WONDER WHAT HAPPENS IF YOU THROW UP IN ZERO GRAVITY.

MAYBE YOU SHOULD WONDER WHAT IT'S LIKE TO WALK HOME.

HANG ON! WE'RE COMING IN THROUGH MARS' ATMOSPHERE.

BONK BONK

WE'VE LANDED! WE'RE THE FIRST ONES TO EVER SET FOOT ON ANOTHER PLANET! WHAT A HISTORIC MOMENT!

I STILL CAN'T BELIEVE YOU FORGOT THE CAMERA.

I REMEMBERED IT. YOU JUST DIDN'T WANT TO TURN AROUND.

SEE ANY SIGNS OF MARTIAN LIFE?

NOT YET...

HEY, LOOK! IT'S THE OLD "VIKING" SPACECRAFT THAT LANDED HERE IN THE '70s!

GOSH, I WONDER IF IT'S STILL WORKING.

BLAHHHH HOOP HOOP BOOLA ACKACKACK BOOLA

THAT OUGHT TO BLOW SOME CIRCUITS AT NASA!

HEE HEE HEE! I'VE ALWAYS WANTED TO DO SOMETHING LIKE THAT.

FOR SHOW AND TELL, I BROUGHT A SPACE ALIEN I CAPTURED IN MY BACK YARD.

YES, FOR THE LAST TWO DAYS I'VE BEEN KEEPING IT IN THIS SPECIAL ZARNIUM-COATED BAG, AND FEEDING IT PURE AMMONIA!

AND NOW, THE MOMENT YOU'VE ALL BEEN WAITING FOR!

AARGH!

HOW'D IT WORK?

MY TEACHER SAYS MOM AND DAD BOTH HAVE TO SIGN MY REPORT CARDS THIS YEAR.

SCOOTCH SCOOTCH

GREETINGS. I AM AN X-387 ROBOT PROBE SENT FROM JUPITER.

MM HMM.

MY SENSORS INDICATE TRACE AMOUNTS OF CHOCOLATE IN THE PANTRY. PLEASE LOAD SOME IN MY SCOOP FOR ANALYSIS.

NO, YOU'LL SPOIL YOUR APPETITE.

MY MISSION MUST NOT FAIL. PREPARE FOR ANNIHILATION, PITIFUL EARTH FEMALE.

GO BACK TO JUPITER, X-3 WHATEVER.

YOU KNOW, WHEN YOU THINK ABOUT IT, OUR LIVES ARE PRETTY NICE.

A LOT OF KIDS DON'T HAVE AS GOOD OF A HOME LIFE AS WE DO. WE REALLY CAN'T COMPLAIN.

..WHICH ISN'T TO SAY WE SHOULD GO HOME YET.

WHEN DO YOU THINK THEY'LL SEE THE CAR WINDSHIELD?

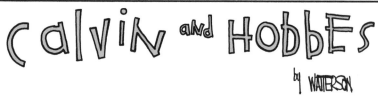

Calvin and Hobbes
by WATTERSON

YOU KNOW WHAT WOULD MAKE THIS HOUSE A LOT BETTER?

NO, WHAT?

YOU SHOULD TAKE OUT THE STAIRS AND PUT IN AN ELEVATOR.

GOOD. I'LL FILE THAT WITH YOUR IDEA FOR THE MOVING SIDEWALK.

OH NO!

WHOAAA

OWW

..WWCH!

WHOAAA

OWW

..WWCH!

WHOAAA

OWW

..WWCH!

DID YOU FALL DOWN THE STAIRS AGAIN?!

THAT'S ME (OOF) THE HUMAN SLINKY.

CALViN and HobbEs

by WATTERSON

UH-OH.

SOMETHING IS VERY WRONG HERE.

CALVIN HAS MYSTERIOUSLY SHRUNK TO A QUARTER OF AN INCH TALL!

HOW CAN HE MAKE HIS PLIGHT KNOWN TO HIS PARENTS WHEN HE'S SMALLER THAN A PENNY?

CALVIN GETS AN IDEA! HE GRABS THE LEG OF A PASSING HOUSEFLY AND FLIES TO HIS DAD'S CAMERA!

ONCE THERE, HE CLIMBS UP AND SETS THE SELF-TIMER.

JUMPING ON THE SHUTTER, CALVIN HAS FIFTEEN SHORT SECONDS TO GET IN FRONT OF THE LENS!

WITH LUCK, CALVIN'S DAD WILL HAVE THE FILM DEVELOPED SOON, AND DISCOVER WHAT HAS HAPPENED!

WHAT HAPPENED?! LOOK AT ALL THESE TERRIBLE PICTURES! I DON'T REMEMBER TAKING THESE. WHO'S THAT LITTLE SPECK IN THE DISTANCE ALL THE TIME? YOU HAVEN'T BEEN FOOLING WITH MY CAMERA, HAVE YOU?

ME? HECK, NO. MAYBE YOU SHOULD GET THE CAMERA FIXED.

I THINK THE WORST OF THIS IS OVER, SO JUST TRY TO GET SOME SLEEP.

I'M GOING BACK TO BED, BUT GIVE ME A CALL IF YOU FEEL SICK AGAIN, OK? NOW GET SOME REST.

MM HMM.

POOR LITTLE KID.

YECCHHH! THERE IS NOTHING WORSE THAN A SICK ROOMMATE! FACE THAT WAY!

IT'S SCARY BEING SICK... ESPECIALLY AT NIGHT.

WHAT IF SOMETHING IS REALLY WRONG WITH ME, AND I HAVE TO GO TO THE HOSPITAL??

WHAT IF THEY STICK ME FULL OF TUBES AND HOSES? WHAT IF THEY HAVE TO OPERATE? WHAT IF THE OPERATION FAILS? WHAT IF THIS IS MY... MY... LAST NIGHT... ALIVE??

THEN I CAN LOOK FORWARD TO HAVING THE BED TO MYSELF TOMORROW.

FEW THINGS ARE LESS COMFORTING THAN A TIGER WHO'S UP TOO LATE.

FEELING ANY BETTER THIS MORNING, CALVIN?

NO.

I GUESS I'D BETTER MAKE YOU AN APPOINTMENT WITH THE DOCTOR.

OK.

IT'S SATURDAY, BY THE WAY. YOU WON'T MISS SCHOOL.

I KNOW.

WELL, IT LOOKS LIKE CALVIN JUST CAUGHT THE BUG GOING AROUND. NOTHING SERIOUS.

KEEP AN EYE ON HIM, AND LET ME KNOW IF HE ISN'T FEELING BETTER SOON.

OK. THANK YOU.

SO LONG, CALVIN. YOU WERE A GOOD PATIENT THIS TIME.

MM.

NOTHING LIKE A LITTLE VIRUS TO TAKE THE EDGE OFF A KID.

I'D STILL RATHER LET HIS TEACHER DEAL WITH HIM.

I GET TO STAY HOME FROM SCHOOL TODAY.

I GET TO LIE IN BED, DRINK TEA, AND READ COMIC BOOKS ALL DAY.

I WISH I COULD DO THIS EVERY DAY.

...LIKE SOME PEOPLE I KNOW.

YOUR MOM DOESN'T BRING *ME* TEA IN BED.

I WANT SOME MORE TOAST.

ROOM SERVICE!!

HA! *THAT* SURE GOT YOU UP HERE QUICK!

TOMORROW YOU'RE GOING TO SCHOOL.

I THINK PEOPLE WORRY TOO MUCH ABOUT LITTLE THINGS.

ALL THEY DO IS MAKE THEMSELVES UNHAPPY THAT WAY.

WHY GET AN ULCER OVER THINGS THAT DON'T REALLY MATTER?

LIKE THE BOOK REPORT YOU'RE SUPPOSED TO BE WRITING NOW ON THE BOOK YOU HAVEN'T READ?

EXACTLY. CASE IN POINT.

WHY IN THE WORLD AM I WAITING IN THE POURING RAIN FOR THE SCHOOL BUS TO TAKE ME SOMEWHERE I DON'T EVEN WANT TO GO?

I GO TO SCHOOL, BUT I NEVER LEARN WHAT I WANT TO KNOW.

I HATE SCHOOL.

EACH DAY I COUNT THE HOURS UNTIL SCHOOL'S OVER. THEN I COUNT THE DAYS UNTIL THE WEEKEND. THEN I COUNT THE WEEKS UNTIL THE MONTH IS OVER, AND THEN THE MONTHS UNTIL SUMMER.

I ALWAYS HAVE TO POSTPONE WHAT I *WANT* TO DO FOR WHAT I *HAVE* TO DO!

WELCOME TO THE WORLD.

WOULD YOU SIGN THIS PARENTAL EXCUSE TO GET ME OUT OF THE NEXT 11½ YEARS OF SCHOOL?

235

Calvin and Hobbes

by Watterson

THE VALIANT SPACEMAN SPIFF, INTERGALACTIC EXPLORER, COMES IN OVER THE MOUNTAINS OF A STRANGE PLANET!

OUR HERO DESPERATELY HOPES TO FIND A REST AREA WITH WORKING FACILITIES.

SPACEMAN SPIFF LANDS ON THE DISTANT PLANET ZOKK!

CLIMBING DOWN FROM HIS SPACECRAFT, OUR HERO PREPARES TO EXPLORE THE SURFACE!

UNEXPECTEDLY, SPIFF'S FIRST STEP SENDS HIM CAREENING THROUGH THE SKY!

SPIFF QUICKLY REALIZES THAT PLANET ZOKK HAS ONLY A FRACTION OF EARTH'S GRAVITY!

OOF

WITH PRACTICE, OUR HERO SOON FINDS HE CAN BOUND EFFORTLESSLY ACROSS THE LANDSCAPE!

STOP BOUNCING ON THE BED AND GO TO SLEEP!

DUMB BALLOON.

POOF POOF

POOF POOOF

POOFF

HEY, SUSIE, DID YOU HAVE ANY TROUBLE WITH OUR MATH HOMEWORK LAST NIGHT?

NO, WHY?

I THOUGHT A COUPLE OF THESE WERE TRICKY. CAN I CHECK MY ANSWERS WITH YOURS?

OK.

THANKS. WHAT DID YOU GET FOR QUESTION ONE?

SEVEN.

SEVEN? GOOD, THAT'S WHAT I GOT. WHAT DID YOU GET FOR QUESTION TWO?

DROP DEAD, CALVIN.

EVER SIT AND WATCH ANTS?

LOOK AT THIS ONE. HE'S CARRYING A CRUMB THAT'S BIGGER THAN HE IS, AND HE'S *RUNNING*.

AND IF YOU PUT AN OBSTACLE IN FRONT OF HIM, HE'LL SCRAMBLE LIKE CRAZY UNTIL HE GETS ACROSS IT. HE DOESN'T LET ANYTHING STOP HIM.

I JUST CAN'T IDENTIFY WITH THAT KIND OF WORK ETHIC.

CaLViN and HObbEs

by WATTERSON

CALVIN, TAKE OFF YOUR OUTFIT BEFORE YOU SIT AT THE TABLE, OK?

CALVIN? WHO'S CALVIN? I'M *STUPENDOUS MAN!*

STOP BEING SILLY, AND DO AS I ASKED YOU.

BUT MOM, I *NEED* TO WEAR THIS FOR DINNER!

NO YOU DON'T. LET'S GO.

BUT STUPENDOUS MAN HAS A STOMACH OF STEEL!

MOM SAID I CAN'T GO OUTSIDE UNTIL I FINISH MY HOMEWORK. IF YOU'LL HELP ME, I'LL BE DONE FASTER. WHAT'S FIVE PLUS SEVEN?

I DON'T KNOW.

I DON'T EITHER.

THEN WRITE, "I DON'T KNOW."

HEY, THAT'S A TRUE ANSWER, ISN'T IT! I CAN WRITE THAT FOR *ALL* OF THESE! WE'RE DONE!

WE'D BETTER HAVE A LOOK AT OUR PRODIGY'S HOMEWORK.

WANT TO GO PLAY OUTSIDE?

NO. I'M WATCHING TV.

YOU HATE THIS SHOW. LET'S GO OUT.

NAH.

WHY NOT?

DAD FINALLY SAID HE WAS SICK OF ARGUING WITH ME, AND FOR ALL HE CARED, I COULD WATCH TV UNTIL MY BRAINS OOZED OUT MY EARS.

SO YOU'RE GOING TO?

IT WAS A HARD-WON PRIVILEGE.

WELL DAD, WE'RE RIGHT DOWN TO THE WIRE, AND THE POLLS SAY YOU WON'T BE DAD HERE MUCH LONGER.

IT SEEMS YOU'RE JUST NOT LIKEABLE ENOUGH. THOSE POLLED CONTINUE TO FIND YOU A COLD FISH.

IF YOU WANT SOME ADVICE, I'D SUGGEST YOU DO SOMETHING EXTRAORDINARILY LIKEABLE IN THE NEXT TWO MINUTES.

GO TO BED.

NO, NO! IT'S *WAY* TOO LATE TO LEARN HOW TO TELL JOKES.

TEN... FIFTEEN... SIX... TWENTY-TWO...

HIKE!

YAAAA

AUGH!

ANOTHER FIVE YARD LOSS!

WE'VE GOT TO GET SOME OTHER PLAYERS.

BOY, YOU'RE LUCKY *YOU* DON'T HAVE TO GO TO SCHOOL LIKE *I* DO.

YOU DON'T KNOW WHAT IT'S LIKE TO GET UP ON THESE COLD, DARK MORNINGS AND HAVE TO GO SOMEPLACE YOU HATE.

YES I DO.

OH YEAH? HOW COULD YOU?

YOU TELL ME EVERY MORNING.

OH, AM I KEEPING YOU AWAKE?! I'M *SORRY!*

HEY, SUSIE, CAN I BORROW YOUR BLACK CRAYON?

OK, BUT DON'T BREAK IT, AND DON'T PEEL THE PAPER OFF, AND COLOR WITH ALL SIDES OF IT SO IT STAYS POINTY.

GEEZ, WHY DON'T YOU TAKE OUT AN INSURANCE POLICY ON IT?

JUST DON'T RUIN MY CRAYON. WHAT ARE YOU DRAWING ANYWAY?

BLACK BEARS ATTACKING A BLACK FOREST CAMPGROUND AT MIDNIGHT.

GIVE ME MY CRAYON BACK.

HEY! WHAT'S THIS STUFF IN MY SOUP?! YECCHH! IS THIS RICE ?!? IT HAD BETTER *NOT* BE!

RICE? LET ME SEE.

LOOK! THESE LITTLE WHITE THINGS! SEE, THERE'S RICE IN MY SOUP! I HATE RICE!

I DIDN'T PUT ANY RICE IN. THOSE ARE MAGGOTS.

EWWWW!

ANOTHER LOVELY MEAL AT HOME WITH MY FAMILY. ...I WISH MY JOB REQUIRED MORE TRAVEL.

WELL, HE'S *EATING* IT NOW, RIGHT?

GOSH, WAIT 'TIL I TELL EVERYONE AT SCHOOL WHAT *WE* HAD FOR DINNER!

UH OH.

HOOP

EEP!

I'VE GOT THE HICCUPS SOMETHING TERRIBLE, MOM.

DRINK SOME WATER.

WHEN I GROW UP, I WANT TO BE AN INVENTOR. FIRST I WILL INVENT A TIME MACHINE.

THEN I'LL COME BACK TO YESTERDAY

AND TAKE MYSELF TO TOMORROW

AND SKIP THIS DUMB ASSIGNMENT.

MOMMM, I'M HOME FROM SCHOOL! OPEN THE DOOR FOR ME, OK?

WHAT'S THE MATTER? IT WASN'T LOCKED.

SOMETIMES HOBBES IS WAITING TO POUNCE ON ME AS SOON AS I OPEN THE DOOR.

OH FOR HEAVEN'S SAKE! FROM NOW ON, DON'T CALL ME TO COME TO THE DOOR UNLESS IT'S LOCKED.

HA! I SURE OUT-SMARTED HOBBES *THIS* TIME!

THBBPTT!

SISSY.

BOY, I'M IN A BAD MOOD TODAY! EVERYONE HAD BETTER STEER CLEAR OF ME!

I HATE *EVERYBODY!* AS FAR AS I'M CONCERNED, EVERYONE ON THE PLANET CAN JUST DROP DEAD. PEOPLE ARE SCUM.

WELL-L-L? DOESN'T ANYONE WANT TO CHEER ME UP?!?

CALVIN AND HOBBES by WATTERSON

WHO **IS** THIS MYSTERIOUS MASKED MAN??

KAPWIINGG!

AND WHY HAS HE NEVER BEEN PHOTOGRAPHED TOGETHER WITH HANDSOME, 6-YEAR-OLD MILLIONAIRE PLAYBOY CALVIN?

A SOLITARY CAPED FIGURE RUNS ACROSS A MOONLIT BUILDING TOP!

A CRIMSON BOLT BLASTS ACROSS THE NIGHT SKY, STRIKING FEAR INTO THE HEARTS OF ALL EVILDOERS!

YES, IT'S *STUPENDOUS MAN,* CHAMPION OF LIBERTY, DEFENDER OF FREE WILL!

SOME DIABOLICAL FIEND THREATENS TO ESTABLISH A TOTALITARIAN SYSTEM OF RULE! ONLY *STUPENDOUS MAN* CAN SAVE THE DAY!

AHA! JUST AS I SUSPECTED! MY EVIL ARCHNEMESIS, *MOM-LADY!*

DIDN'T I TELL YOU TO GO TO BED?!?

OH, NO! STUPENDOUS MAN'S STUPENDOUS POWERS ARE NO MATCH AGAINST HIS ADVERSARY! STUPENDOUS MAN IS VANQUISHED!

THIS WOULD HAVE BEEN PLENTY HUMILIATING *WITHOUT* THE GOODNIGHT KISS.

AND TAKE OFF THAT SILLY HOOD BEFORE YOU SMOTHER IN YOUR SLEEP.

The End